Honduras

Contents

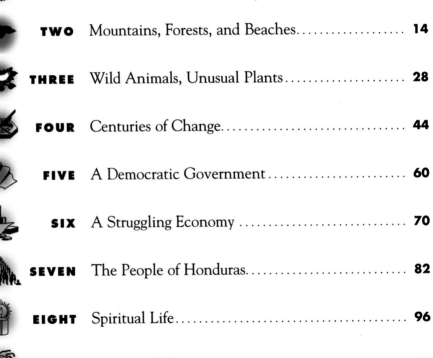

Cover photo:
A Honduran boy
carrying a jug
of water

The Choluteca River

Mayan statue

A Land of Pride

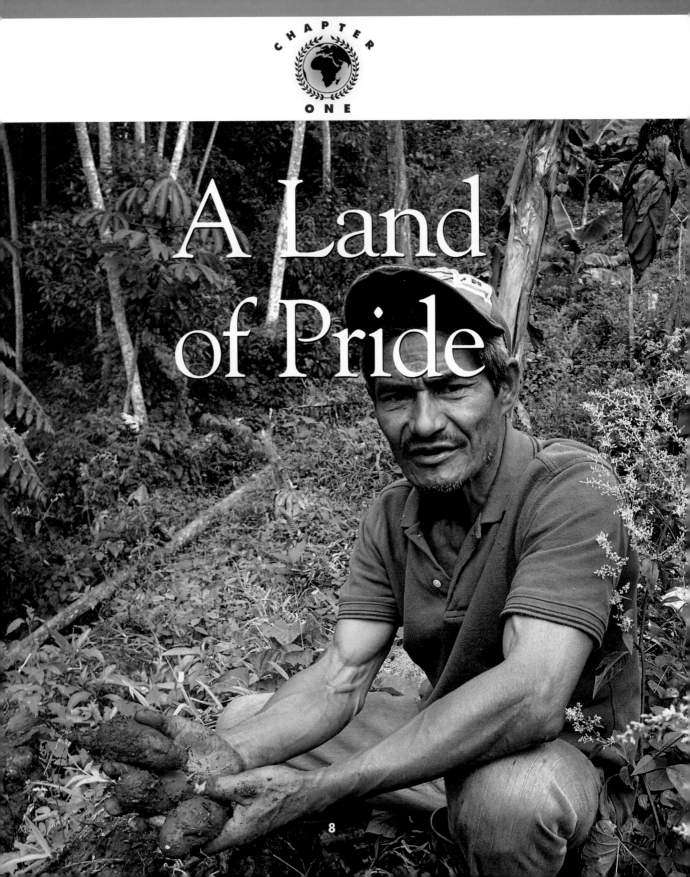

H ONDURAS IS A COUNTRY OF BEAUTIFUL LANDSCAPES. It is filled with high mountains, misty forests, thick jungles, and pristine beaches. In its cities, modern factories hum with activity. In the country, farmers who till small plots of land struggle to survive. The blood of Hondurans is a mix of indigenous peoples, Spanish conquerors, and African slaves.

In ancient times, a Mayan boy running toward the great city of Copán would hear, off in the distance, a howler monkey's loud call echo through the valley. He would hear the roar of a jaguar on the hunt. In the treetops above, a sloth would climb slowly from branch to branch as scarlet macaws and toucans flew by.

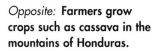

Opposite: **Farmers grow crops such as cassava in the mountains of Honduras.**

The brightly colored beak of the teal-billed toucan grows up to 8 inches (20 cm) long.

By the time the Spanish conquistadores, or conquerors, arrived in this land, the city of Copán was in ruins. Even the native peoples did not know who had once lived there. The Spaniards quickly claimed Honduras as their own. But they would not get the land without a fight. The native people fought against the foreigners for more than two decades.

The Great Plaza was at the center of the Mayan city of Copán, which was once home to twenty thousand people.

Spain ruled Honduras for hundreds of years. Once Honduras gained its independence from Spain, it became an area of constant conflict. Military leaders, frequent battles with neighboring countries, and interference by foreign governments weakened the struggling country. By the end of the nineteenth century, foreign banana companies were taking advantage of Honduran workers, leading the country further into poverty.

Men harvest bananas on a plantation in La Ceiba. In 1910, U.S. companies controlled 80 percent of the banana-growing region of Honduras.

Workers restore a temple at Copán. About 4,500 different structures have been identified among the ruins of the ancient Mayan city.

But the Hondurans would not give up. They demanded free elections and workers' rights. Because of their long fight, Honduras has been democratic for more than twenty years. Labor unions have been established, protecting factory and plantation workers.

Hondurans remain proud of their past. Today, they are working to restore Copán, one of the great Mayan cities, to its

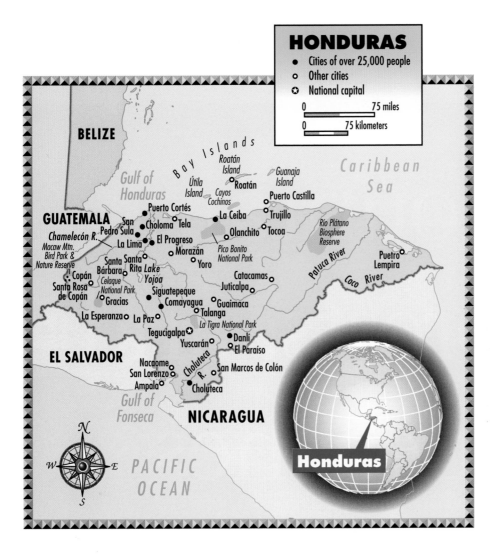

former glory. They are also proud of their present. This is evident in their efforts to conserve the forests and jungles, which they consider national treasures. In national parks and wildlife reserves, a young girl can still hear the roar of a howler monkey and spy the bright beak of a toucan as it flits through the trees. Honduras is a poor country facing many problems, but the pride and determination of its people will help guide the nation steadily forward.

Mountains, Forests, and Beaches

A pile of coconuts lie on the sand near Tela, on the Caribbean coast of Honduras.

Honduras is a mountainous land filled with rain forests and fertile valleys. It is the second-largest country in Central America. Covering 43,277 square miles (112,087 square kilometers), it is slightly larger than the state of Tennessee.

Honduras is shaped like a large triangle. Its northern coast borders the Caribbean Sea, while its southwestern coast borders the Pacific Ocean. On the Caribbean side, it is located between Guatemala and Nicaragua. On the Pacific Ocean, it is wedged between El Salvador and Nicaragua. In addition to the mainland, Honduras also includes the Bay Islands, located in the Caribbean Sea, and islands in the Gulf of Fonseca, an arm of the Pacific Ocean.

Opposite: **Tobacco grows easily in the rich land of the Copán River valley of northwestern Honduras.**

A Long Dispute

For two hundred years, Honduras was involved in a boundary dispute with El Salvador over 169 square miles (437 sq km) of land plus two islands in the Gulf of Fonseca named Meanguera and El Tigre. Besides land, the dispute also involved the right of Honduran ships to pass through the Gulf of Fonseca into the Pacific Ocean.

The dispute started in the eighteenth century when boundaries were not fully defined. During the nineteenth century, many attempts were made to resolve the dispute, but with no success. The argument continued into the twentieth century until a war broke out between the two countries in 1969. Because this war started with violence at a soccer match between the two countries, it became known as the Soccer War.

On October 30, 1980, Honduras and El Salvador finally signed a peace treaty. They also agreed to submit the boundary dispute to the International Court of Justice in the Netherlands if they failed to resolve it themselves within five years. In fact, five years passed without the dispute being resolved, so in 1986, the case was presented before the International Court of Justice. A ruling was made in 1992, and both countries agreed to the decision.

Honduras received 116 square miles (300 sq km) of land and the island of El Tigre. In addition, Honduras was guaranteed free passage to the Pacific Ocean. El Salvador was granted 53 square miles (137 sq km) of land and the island of Meanguera.

Some historians claim that Honduras, which means "depths," got its name from Christopher Columbus. The story goes that a violent storm struck while Columbus and his crew were exploring Honduras. He found a deep bay on the eastern coast to protect his ship. During the storm, Columbus said, "*¡Gracias a Dios que hemos salido de estas honduras!*" Translated this means, "Thank God we've escaped these depths!"

Christopher Columbus steered his ship up to what is now Trujillo, Honduras, in 1502.

Varied Land

Honduras can be divided into four land regions—the interior mountains, the southern coast, the northern coast, and the northeastern plain. More than three-quarters of Honduras is covered with mountains, the most of any Central American country. Mountains dominate the middle of the nation. Swift rivers zigzag through the mountains' pine and rain forests.

Several wide, level valleys called basins cut through the mountains. Beans, cattle, coffee, and corn are raised in these basins. One of the most important basins is the Comayagua Valley. Vegetables such as tomatoes, peppers, squash, and eggplants are grown there for export to the United States and Asia.

Pico Bonito in northern Honduras soars 7,992 feet (2,436 m) into the sky.

Looking at Honduras's Cities

The second-largest city in Honduras is San Pedro Sula (above), which lies in the northwestern part of the country. It is the nation's most industrial and commercial city and is the center of manufacturing and trade. Industries include concrete, shoes, plastics, steel, and textiles. One of the best museums in the country, the Museum of Anthropology and History, is located in San Pedro Sula. In 2005, the city had an estimated population of 489,466.

Comayagua, the most important city of colonial Honduras, was founded in 1537. Once Honduras became independent from Spain in 1821, a power struggle ensued between Comayagua and Tegucigalpa as to which would become the capital of the country. For almost sixty years, the two cities alternated

each year as the capital. In 1880, Tegucigalpa was named the permanent capital of Honduras. Because Comayagua was the center of government for many years, it has many colonial landmarks and buildings. Some of these old monuments are crumbling, but the government, with help from Spain, has started a program to return them to their original state. In 2005, Comayagua had a population of 58,784.

La Ceiba, Honduras's third-largest city, is located along the Caribbean coast at the base of the soaring mountain called Pico Bonito. It is the commercial center for the Standard Fruit Company, which grows pineapples and bananas. La Ceiba had a population of 130,218 in 2005. When Hurricane Fifi hit the city in 1974, more than a thousand people were killed.

The Choluteca River winds through the fertile valleys of southern Honduras.

On the flat Pacific coastal plain, cotton, melons, and sugar-cane are grown. Cattle are also raised there. The Choluteca River enters the Pacific in the Gulf of Fonseca. Most locals fish for a living. Over the last several years, shrimp farming has become a very lucrative business in the gulf. The country's third-largest port, Puerto Henecan, is on the Pacific coast.

The Man Who Mapped Honduras

A Honduran named Jesús Aguilar Paz began exploring his country in 1912. He traveled on mule, camping as he went. He decided to map Honduras without official support. After twenty years of exploring Honduras, he made a very detailed map in 1933. Years later, in 2000, mapmakers from the United States Geological Survey went to Honduras to remake the map. Very little of Paz's original map needed to be changed.

Several islands located in the Gulf of Fonseca are also part of Honduras. The two largest are Isla del Tigre and Isla Zacate Grande. (*Isla* is a Spanish word meaning "island.") They are ancient volcanoes that are no longer active. Up until 1770, Isla del Tigre was used as a hideout by pirates.

There is more human activity on Honduras's Caribbean coast than on its Pacific coast. Its rich river valleys make excellent farmland. Pineapples, lemons, oranges, sugarcane, and bananas are grown to be sold locally and exported. Puerto Cortés, the main port of Honduras, and Puerto Castilla, the second-largest port, are both on the Caribbean coast.

Oranges are among the leading crops in Honduras.

Fish Raining from the Sky?

In north-central Honduras is a province called Yoro, which has an unusual story. Occasionally, Yoro has experienced cloudbursts where fish literally rain from the sky. It is thought that a waterspout in the Caribbean Sea carries the fish up into the clouds. They then drop to the ground farther inland in Yoro.

Farther east on the northeastern plain is an area with few people. It is called the Mosquito Coast. Inland, it has grassland with thick, tropical, hot, humid rain forests. Toward the coast are swamps and lagoons where mangrove trees grow from the salty water. Several indigenous groups live in small villages on the Mosquito Coast. During heavy rainfall, the grasslands are flooded. The local people use canoes and flat-bottom boats for transportation.

The northeastern coast is the least populated part of Honduras. The thick forests and swampy land make it difficult to get around.

About 38 miles (61 km) off the Caribbean coast are the Bay Islands. They are Roatán, Útila, Guanaja, and the Cayos Cochinos (Hog Keys). Formed by earthquakes and volcanoes, the Bay Islands have mountains sloping down to beautiful white beaches with clear blue waters. Roatán is the largest of the Bay Islands. It is 31 miles (50 km) long and 3 miles (5 km) wide.

The Bay Islands have a colorful history. Over the years, they have been visited by Spanish conquistadores, slave traders, indigenous peoples, and pirates. Today, divers from all over the world visit the Bay Islands to explore the pristine coral reef off its shores where colorful fish thrive.

Honduras's Geographic Features

Area: 43,277 square miles (112,087 sq km)

Largest Lake: Lake Yojoa

Longest Coastline: Caribbean Sea, 382 miles (615 km)

Lowest Elevation: Sea level along the coasts

Highest Elevation: Cerro Las Minas, at 9,347 feet (2,849 m)

Longest River: Coco River, 485 miles (780 km)

Longest Border: 573 miles (922 km), with Nicaragua

Greatest Annual Rainfall: 100 inches (254 cm) in the Caribbean coastal region

Lowest Annual Rainfall: 30 inches (76 cm) in the central highlands

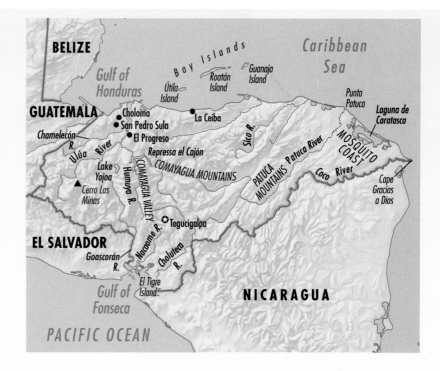

Many rushing waterfalls grace the mountains of Honduras.

Waterways

Most rivers in Honduras flow into the Caribbean Sea. The Coco River is the nation's longest and is shared with neighboring Nicaragua, creating a natural border. It flows through the forest of the Mosquito Coast. Honduras's second-longest river is the Patuca, which has dramatic waterfalls and is surrounded by densely forested mountains. The Ulúa River and the Chamelecón River converge, draining into the northern Sula Valley. On the Pacific coast, the Choluteca, Nacaome, and Goascorán rivers flow into the ocean.

The largest natural lake in Honduras is Lake Yojoa. It is 14 miles long (23 km) and as much as 9 miles (14 km) wide. The lake is located between the capital, Tegucigalpa, and San Pedro Sula. Surrounding the lake are mountains soaring to the sky. In the mountains, many kinds of animals thrive, including jaguars, anteaters, and howler monkeys. Lake Yojoa itself is home to more than 373 species of birds. Three national parks have been set up in the lake area to help protect the wildlife.

Lake Yojoa is famed for its bird-watching and bass fishing.

Climate

There are two seasons in Honduras. The dry season runs from November through April, and the rainy season runs from May through October. During the rainy season, the southern and central highlands can get up to 60 inches (152 centimeters) of rain. But the Mosquito Coast, which has thick tropical rain forests, receives more than 100 inches (250 cm) of rain over the course of the year.

Because Honduras's land is so varied, it has many climates. Honduras is generally warm year-round. Even so, depending on the location, temperatures can fluctuate widely.

The northern coast is the rainiest part of Honduras. Here, a man in La Ceiba surveys his yard after a heavy rain.

Hurricanes in Honduras

Honduras suffers frequent hurricanes. In 1969, it was hit by Hurricane Francelia, and in 1982, by Tropical Storm Alleta. Both storms caused massive crop damage. One of the nation's worst hurricanes struck in 1974, when Hurricane Fifi killed eight thousand people and wiped out the entire banana crop.

Even worse was Hurricane Mitch, which struck Honduras in 1998. Mitch ripped up roads, bridges, and entire villages. The hurricane caused massive flooding. Cars swept up in the floodwaters were piled on top of each other like toy blocks. In some places, the water completely submerged school buses, and houses were washed away. People huddled on rooftops to be rescued while the menacing water rose around them. Mudslides

pushed entire villages down cliffs. The storm knocked out radio, TV, and telephone service, leaving people totally isolated. By the time the storm passed and Hondurans were able to take stock of what had happened, nine thousand people were dead. Another 1.5 million were left homeless. Mitch was the deadliest hurricane in Honduran history.

The coastal lowlands are warm and humid. The average temperature throughout the year there is about 88 degrees Fahrenheit (31 degrees Celsius). In the mountains near Tegucigalpa, the air is cooler and drier. The average yearly temperature in the mountains is 74°F (23°C). But during May, the hottest month, temperatures can rise above 90°F (32°C), and during December, the coldest month, temperatures can go below 50°F (10°C).

The northern coast and the Bay Islands are consistently hot and humid. Rain falls throughout the year. The Pacific coast experiences high temperatures but has a drier climate than the Caribbean coast.

Wild Animals, Unusual Plants

Ａ WIDE VARIETY OF ANIMALS POPULATE HONDURAS'S many landscapes. And the country's mountain slopes, fertile valleys, and thick jungles support an abundance of plants.

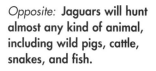

Opposite: **Jaguars will hunt almost any kind of animal, including wild pigs, cattle, snakes, and fish.**

Jungle Animals

Honduras has three types of monkeys—spider monkeys, white-faced capuchins, and howler monkeys. The howler monkey gets its name from its loud call, which can be heard up to 3 miles (5 km) away. It can grow up to 4 feet (1.2 meters) tall and weigh up to 22 pounds (10 kilograms). Its neck and jaw are large, to support its big vocal cords.

White-faced capuchins are smart and lively. Fruit such as mangoes, guavas, and papayas are the mainstay of their diet.

Sleek, majestic cougars and jaguars live deep in the jungle. Jaguars are strong hunters. They can bring down a cow and have been known to kill and eat alligators. A jaguar's fur is gold with black spots, and the animal can grow to lengths of 5 to 6 feet (1.5 to 1.8 m), excluding its 3-foot (1 m) tail.

Many other creatures spend much of their time in the treetops. Coatis, which are related to raccoons, climb from branch to branch in troops of up to twenty. The coati's snout is long, and the animal has an excellent sense of smell. Iguanas, large lizards that sometimes reach 6 feet (1.8 m), also live in the trees. On the Pacific coast of Honduras, iguana eggs are

An iguana's tail makes up about half its body length. The iguana sometimes fends off attacks by using its tail to whip the other creatures.

The National Mammal

Honduras's national mammal is the Yucatan white-tailed deer. This deer can be found both on the country's plains and in its pine forests. It feeds mainly on herbs, fruit, and other types of wild vegetation. Cougars, jaguars, and humans all prey on the Yucatan white-tailed deer. The deer has an amazing sense of smell and is a strong swimmer, both of which help protect it from these threats. When the animal senses danger, it raises its white tail like a flag and runs.

considered to be a delicacy. Hondurans also sometimes catch iguanas to make a nice meal. To catch an iguana, a banana is placed on a hook and put out as a lure. When the iguana bites the banana, it is caught on the hook like a fish.

Down on the ground, armadillos, raccoons, opossums, and agoutis thrive. An agouti is a rodent that is related to the guinea pig. When the agouti first senses danger, it freezes. It sits upright and then lets out a sharp scream while scampering away. The agouti is a common prey for the jaguar.

Baird's tapirs look big and awkward, but they are actually quite agile. They can easily climb up steep mountainsides.

The largest mammal native to Honduras is the Baird's tapir. Almost the size of a donkey, the Baird's tapir weighs up to 800 pounds (360 kg). Its nose looks like a pig's snout. It uses its snout to stuff leaves into its small mouth. These mammals live near water. If they are disturbed while on land, they rush quickly toward water, trampling anything in their way.

Though Honduras has a wide variety of animals, they are often difficult to see. Partly this is because they are good at hiding. But it is also because their numbers have dwindled as the forests where they live have been cut down and the animals have been overhunted.

Domestic Animals

Many families in Honduras keep animals such as cows, horses, donkeys, goats, and oxen. Oxen are sometimes used in rural areas to pull wagons or carts filled with goods. Horses are also used to get from place to place. Cats and dogs are familiar family pets. But the most common animals in villages are chickens. Children often have chickens as pets. In some villages, chickens are kept in coops during the night. During the day, the chickens may roam free, scratching the dirt for feed. In other villages, chickens are allowed to roam both day and night. Some rural homes have dirt floors, and chickens go in and out of them freely.

Oxen are used to pull heavy loads over the rough Honduran land.

Honduras has a huge variety of insects. Some are beautiful and interesting. Others can be annoying and even life-threatening. Mosquitoes are found pretty much everywhere in Honduras, especially during the rainy season. These mosquitoes can transmit malaria, a sometimes deadly disease that causes chills and fever. Visitors to Honduras must take malaria medication during their entire stay. Some mosquitoes in Honduras also carry the virus that causes dengue fever. Each year, dengue fever strikes thousands of Hondurans, causing fever, rash, and—sometimes—deadly bleeding.

A man sprays a house with poison to kill the mosquitoes during an outbreak of dengue fever. The disease causes high fevers, up to 105°F (41°C).

The bright orange Julia butterfly is a fast flier. It can often be found on the edge of clearings.

Other irritating insects are sand flies on the Bay Islands and ticks in the mountain regions. Both of these small insects have an annoying bite.

One of the most beautiful insects in Honduras is the butterfly. The blue morpho butterfly is almost the size of an adult hand and has shimmering turquoise wings. The zebra butterfly is striped yellow and black, and the Julia is entirely orange. Queen butterflies are also orange but have yellow dots scattered on their wings. Butterflies can be seen in Honduran jungles and forests, but they are also raised on farms. When these butterflies are pupae, the stage between caterpillar and adult, they are sold around the world.

Honduras is home to many types of snakes. The most feared are the fer-de-lance and the coral snake, because their bites can be deadly. Several types of vipers, including the eyelash viper, the jumping viper, and the rain forest hog-nosed viper, are also venomous.

The Montezuma oropendola builds a huge hanging nest. Often, hundreds of these birds will build nests in the same tree.

Birds of Honduras

Honduras is home to a vast array of brightly colored birds. More than seven hundred different bird species live in Honduras. These include woodpeckers, robins, jays, quails, ducks, cuckoos, and parakeets. Hummingbirds of all colors buzz through the air, and yellowed-faced toucans fly from tree to tree. The toucan's bill is often multicolored green, orange, and red. The birds' huge bills are used to pluck fruit, their favorite food. Toucans also down the occasional lizard, spider, or termite.

Montezuma oropendolas have orange-tipped beaks and yellow tails. Trees in the Pico Bonito jungle are decorated with their elaborate hanging nests.

The quetzal lives in Honduras but is difficult to find. It is considered one of the country's most beautiful birds. Males have a bright red breast with dazzling blue-green feathers covering the rest of its body. The quetzal's shimmering green tail feathers can grow up to 3 feet (1 m) long. These birds are usually found in high forests and can be identified by their deep calls.

In a forest next to Copán is Macaw Mountain Bird Park and Nature Reserve, which is home to eighteen species of birds. Multicolored parrots, green toucans, and scarlet macaws live in the reserve. The scarlet macaw is the national bird of Honduras. This huge parrot is red, yellow, blue, and green. They fly in pairs or small groups and make loud, hoarse noises.

Scarlet macaws are a type of parrot. These noisy birds grow to be 35 inches (90 cm) long.

Animals of the Sea

Off the Bay Islands is the Mesoamerican Reef, the world's second-largest coral reef. Many types of sharks prowl the waters near this reef. These include hammerheads, nurse sharks, blacktip sharks, and whale sharks. The whale shark is the largest fish in the world. It can grow to lengths of almost 60 feet (18 m) and can weigh over 20 tons (18 metric tons). It has a 4-foot-wide (1.2 m wide) mouth, which is lined with small teeth. It feeds on plankton and small fish.

Coral reefs are filled with colorful life. Here, cup corals, tunicates, and other species grow on a sunken ship.

Small, colorful fish such as butterflyfish, yellowtail snapper, and angelfish swim near the shore. Hidden in the coral reefs are seahorses, octopuses, sea turtles, and eels. Eagle rays and manta rays glide through the sea looking like underwater birds. Schools of larger fish such as mackerel, tuna, marlin, and kingfish also swim in nearby waters.

Spotlight parrotfish, which live among the coral around Honduras, change sex over the course of their life. They start out as females and later becomes males.

An Underwater Biological Reserve

Cayos Cochinos was declared a biological reserve by the Honduran government in 1993. It's composed of two main islands and several smaller islands. These islands are fringed by clean, white, sandy beaches.

Underwater is a colorful reef filled with beautiful fish and other sea life. Because the reef is protected, it is illegal to anchor a boat there and no commercial fishing is allowed.

Forests cover about half of Honduras. Evergreens grow on the mountaintops.

Plant Life

Honduras's mountains are covered in forest. Red and white pine, oak, and maple trees dominate on the slopes below 7,000 feet (2,100 m). At higher elevations are cloud forests. Cloud forests are areas of forest that are usually covered in clouds. By capturing water from the clouds that would not fall as rain, they help water the rest of Honduras. The cloud forests are made up of evergreen trees and plentiful moss, vines, orchids, and ferns. Honduras has almost forty cloud forests, more than any other country in Central America. The largest of these misty forests have been made into national parks.

Much coffee is grown in the mountains of Honduras. Coffee bushes are planted on mountain slopes shaded by larger

The National Flower

For many years, the national flower of Honduras was the rose, but the rose is not native to Honduras. For this reason, the national flower was changed on November 26, 1969, to an orchid called Brassavola digbiana, which is from Honduras. This flower is known for its unusual beauty and strength. The government has taken measures to protect the orchid where it grows and to teach children how to care for it and grow it in local schools.

trees such as banana trees. Often, entire families help pick and husk the ripened coffee beans. In some villages, the school year is based on the coffee-growing season. Schools are shut down and children are picked up in large trucks and taken to the coffee fields to pick the beans. In many rural areas, children bring their farm tools with them to school so they can work in the fields on the way home. Many schools also have gardens that children help tend so they can learn about agriculture.

The northeastern plain is covered with tropical rain forests. Mahogany, strangler fig, oak, and rosewood are common in these wet forests. The grasslands on the northeastern plain are dotted with pine and palm trees.

A boy rakes coffee beans that have been drying in the sun. Coffee makes up about a fifth of all Honduran exports.

National Parks

Honduras has thirteen national parks. One of them, Celaque, which means "box of water," lives up to its name, for it holds the beginnings of eleven rivers. The park's mountains are filled with dense vegetation that blocks the sun's rays. Water drips from towering trees covered with ferns, vines, and moss. This national park claims the highest peak in the country, Cerro Las Minas.

La Tigra Cloud Forest is located just outside Tegucigalpa. It was declared a national park in 1980. Visitors can follow a trail up into the cloud forest, where tall trees are covered with vines and orchids.

Pico Bonito National Park (below) features tropical broadleaf forests, lush cloud forests, waterfalls, and natural pools.

The northern coast consists of grasslands and swamps, along with palm and pine forest. This is the banana-growing area of Honduras. The soil is rich, and the climate is hot and damp—perfect for banana crops. The word *banana* comes from the Arabic word *banan*, meaning "finger." Bananas are not originally from Honduras. Instead, they were brought there hundreds of years ago from Africa by the Portuguese. Outside of San Pedro Sula, many banana plantations still grow bananas for American fruit companies such as Dole.

Cacao trees also grow in the area. The Maya believed that cacao was brought directly to the earth by the gods. Cacao trees flower two to three times a year. The large, oval fruit pod grows from the trunk or branches of the tree. Once ripe, the pods are cracked open to collect twenty to sixty thin-skinned seeds. Chocolate is made from the processed seeds.

Bananas hang ready to be sorted and shipped. Bananas are Honduras's most valuable crop.

Centuries of Change

EOPLE HAVE LIVED IN WHAT IS NOW HONDURAS FOR thousands of years. As far back as 8000 B.C., small groups of people roamed across the region. They hunted game and gathered fruits, seeds, and nuts. At one point, they stopped roaming and settled in one place. Agriculture soon followed. The oldest artifacts found in Honduras date back to 3000 B.C. Cave art dating back to 2000 B.C. has been found outside of Tegucigalpa. Over the centuries, many different indigenous, or native, groups developed in Honduras. The most powerful were the Maya.

Opposite: **At Copán, the Maya carved statues of their rulers and other important people.**

This head of a shaman is one of many huge carved figures uncovered at the ruins of Copán.

The Maya

The Maya had one of the greatest civilizations in the Americas. The Mayan world spread across what is now southern Mexico, Belize, Guatemala, and El Salvador. By the fifth century A.D., Mayan civilization had reached western Honduras. There the Maya built a city called Copán. The city was filled with temples and pyramids. In time, Copán became a center of Mayan culture.

Copán Ruins

Copán was one of the ancient Maya's southernmost cities. Some historians think that Copán was the Maya's most beautiful city. Within its walls was a ceremonial center with plazas, altars, and ornate pyramids that had temples on top. Sixteen kings ruled Copán during its four hundred years of existence. Royal portraits were carved into stone monuments.

The Maya also carved writing into stone. The Mayan writing system used pictures to represent words. This is called hieroglyphics. Mayan hieroglyphics revealed the history and religion of Copán. For example, Mayan writings mention the many gods the Maya worshiped, including the gods of fire, rain, and corn. A staircase with more than 1,250 hieroglyphic blocks was built into one temple. No other Mayan structure contains so many. Scientists continue studying these stone pictures today.

During its height, the population of Copán swelled to more than 27,500. Trade was established all the way into central Mexico. Scientists, priests, and merchants flocked to the city.

Copán was abandoned in the 800s. Spanish conquistadores discovered its ruins hundreds of years later, in the 1500s. But it wasn't until the American explorer and diplomat John Lloyd Stephens arrived in 1839 and then wrote a book about his travels that the rest of the world became aware of this treasure. Today, tourists and scientists travel from all over the world to explore and view the splendors of this ancient Mayan city.

The Maya were skilled at astronomy. Copán may have been the place where the Maya discovered that the planets rotate around the sun. Mayan astronomers also predicted solar eclipses.

Eventually, Copán began to decline. This may have begun because its population grew too large. The Maya had cut down the surrounding trees for lumber and farmland. Without the trees, the soil on the mountains washed away more easily. During this time, the climate also began to change. Droughts combined with disastrous flooding became common. The Maya began to suffer from malnutrition and disease. In the 800s, Copán was abandoned by priests, rulers, and the educated class. Even so, some people remained. Copán eventually fell into ruin and as time went by, those who remained did not know what had happened to the once magnificent city.

After the Mayan culture collapsed in Honduras, several groups emerged there. They spoke a variety of languages, some of them related to the languages of the Aztecs in Mexico and the Chibchas of Colombia. Some of these languages even included words spoken by Native Americans in what is now the southwestern United States. Some groups, like the Lenca of west-central Honduras, spoke a language unlike any other in the area. Even though the groups spoke different languages and had many conflicts, they still continued to trade with one another.

Spanish Conquistadores

Christopher Columbus first arrived in the Americas in 1492. Ten years later, he made his fourth trip to the Americas,

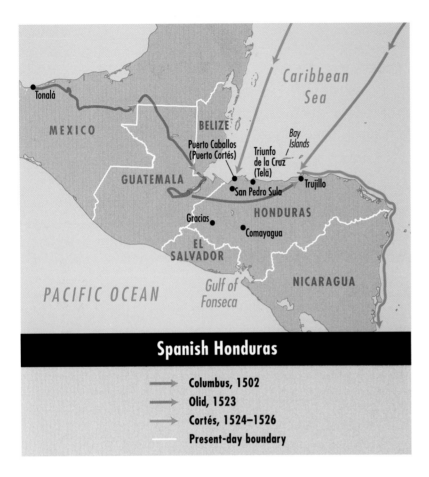

Spanish Honduras

→ Columbus, 1502
→ Olid, 1523
→ Cortés, 1524–1526
— Present-day boundary

landing in Honduras on July 30, 1502. He immediately claimed the territory for Spain. Even so, Spain did not take an interest in Honduras until 1524, when Hernán Cortés, who was in Cuba, an island in the Caribbean, organized a regiment led by Cristóbal de Olid to explore Honduras. Once Olid arrived, he set up a colony and claimed it as his own. When Cortés heard of Olid's treachery, he sent another expedition into Honduras led by Francisco de Las Casas. Olid captured this group. But soon Olid was betrayed by his own men and killed.

Cortés, hearing of the struggle for power in Honduras, decided to go there himself. He soon established a government in the city of Trujillo. He then departed Honduras in 1526 for Mexico. Though the Spanish faced constant peril while in Honduras, they were able to establish three towns: San Pedro Sula, Gracias, and Comayagua. During this time, thousands of indigenous people were killed by Europeans, died from European diseases, or were shipped out of Honduras as slaves.

The Battles of Lempira

In the 1530s, a Lenca chief named Lempira was infuriated by the Spanish occupation and by their treatment of the native people. He convinced a large force of indigenous tribes to join together to fight the Spaniards. After advising them that he planned to get rid of the Spanish invaders, he assembled his army, built a strong fortress, and gathered a large stockpile of supplies. Once they were ready, Lempira gave the signal to attack the Spaniards.

The Spaniards attacked Lempira and his followers, but his fortress could not be penetrated. They fought Lempira for six months and still could not break the Lenca chief's defense. Finally in 1537, the Spaniards killed Lempira. After his death, the other indigenous warriors quickly scattered. The rebellion had been put down. But Lempira's bravery made him a national hero. Today, the Honduran currency is called the lempira in his honor.

A portrait of Lempira appears on the front of the 1-lempira bill. Lempira and his army of thousands of warriors kept the Spaniards at bay for months.

Pirates in the Caribbean

Many pirates sailed the Caribbean Sea in the sixteenth and seventeenth centuries. Some landed in Honduras. One famous pirate, Blackbeard, visited Honduras to meet with another pirate captain, Major Stede Bonnet.

Other pirates hid on the islands off of Honduras. At one point, there were an estimated four thousand pirates in the Caribbean area. Strict laws were passed in England to punish these outlaws.

Spanish Rule

Honduras was ruled by Spain for more than three hundred years. Spain's main interest in Honduras was in the precious minerals that could be found underground. Gold and silver were dug up and shipped off to Spain. Black slaves were brought in from Africa to work in the mines alongside native people. The Spaniards also established cattle ranches to feed the people in the mining towns.

The Spaniards began mining gold soon after they arrived in Honduras. Today, Honduran miners still use pickaxes to dig gold from deep underground.

The United Provinces of Central America

Central America announced its independence from Spain on September 15, 1821. The independent Central American states became part of the Mexican Empire. This relationship ended in 1823 when the United Provinces of Central America was formed. This union consisted of Honduras, Guatemala, El Salvador, Costa Rica, and Nicaragua. The capital was established in Guatemala City, and General Manuel José Arce from El Salvador was named the president.

Tensions soon arose in the United Provinces between two factions, the conservatives and the liberals. The conservatives, who represented the interests of wealthy landowners and the Catholic Church, wanted to continue the values of Spain. The liberals wanted to use the United States as a model for their new government. Because of these disagreements, civil war broke out.

Being a conservative, President Arce attempted to force all liberals from the new government. But a Honduran general, Francisco Morazán, would not stand idly by and watch the federation be overrun with conservatives. He organized an army of Hondurans, Nicaraguans, and Salvadorans and then

United Provinces of Central America

United Provinces of Central America, 1823–1840
Present-day boundary

proceeded to capture Guatemala City in April 1829. President Arce was removed from power, and Morazán was voted in as president of the federation in 1830. President Morazán tried to include more liberal policies in the government, such as reducing the Catholic Church's power, opening trade to foreign countries, and establishing a central government, but his reforms did not take hold.

Honduras's Famous General

Francisco Morazán was born into a mining family in 1792. After the Central American states became independent from Mexico, he joined the army in Tegucigalpa. He worked his way up and was appointed secretary general of Honduras. In 1829, Morazán began his fight to keep the United Provinces of Central America together. He also attempted to make Central America fairer to all its residents. His efforts to reform this system were met with strong opposition.

Morazán became president of the United Provinces of Central America in 1830. When the federation was disbanded in 1838, Morazán fought to keep the Central American countries united. Because of this, he was exiled from Central America in 1840 and fled to Peru. He returned to Costa Rica with an army in 1842 and continued to campaign for reuniting the federation. On September 15, 1842, Morazán was shot by a firing squad in San José, Costa Rica.

American companies ran huge banana plantations on Honduras's northwestern coast. At their peak, bananas accounted for 88 percent of the nation's exports.

Honduras on Its Own

Honduras separated from the United Provinces of Central America in 1838. For the next fifty years, the country developed slowly. There was a coffee boom in Central America in the mid-nineteenth century, but little was grown in Honduras, so it remained poor and underdeveloped. The country had only one library. Its capital city, Tegucigalpa, had no water supply. The city's residents had to carry water by hand from the river. With no running water, getting rid of sewage was a constant problem.

The Caribbean coastal region proved to be a perfect area for growing bananas, however. In 1889, American businessmen called the Vaccaro brothers shipped their first boatload of bananas from Honduras to New Orleans, Louisiana. The fruit sold quickly. The Vaccaro brothers set up a company that eventually became known as the Standard Fruit Company. Bananas began being shipped out of Honduras on a regular basis. The

United Fruit Company and the Cuyamel Fruit Company also began operating in Honduras. Bananas were now being grown and shipped from Honduras in huge numbers.

Yet it was still difficult for Honduras to maintain continuous economic growth. In order to stimulate the economy, Honduran officials gave land grants to North American companies to grow bananas. By 1910, these companies owned the best farming areas along the Caribbean coast. U.S. banana firms and the U.S. government gained great influence over the Honduran government. From 1911 to 1921, U.S. warships were often stationed in the Gulf of Honduras. Presidents were appointed in Honduras who would be sympathetic to the needs of U.S. fruit companies. If the president was not helpful to the banana companies, a coup or revolution was planned and a new president would be appointed. Because of this political relationship, Honduras became known as the "banana republic."

The U.S. fruit companies built railroads to their plantations. They also set up port facilities and equipment. La Ceiba, Tela, Puerto Cortés, La Lima, and towns along the coast were established or strengthened. But the inland towns and cities of Honduras saw very little, if any, of the money made by the sale of bananas in North America. By 1925, Honduras was the world's largest banana producer. Even so, the poverty rate in Honduras remained the same. In the 1930s, a deep economic depression hit the United States. This hurt Honduras because banana exports declined. Many workers on banana plantations lost their jobs or had to take pay cuts.

In 1933, General Tiburcio Carías Andino was elected president. His first order of business was to cancel all elections. Because no one else could be voted into power, he ruled the country as a dictator until 1948. Many who opposed him were treated ruthlessly. During his time in office, labor strikes were ended when soldiers shot protesting workers. He put much of the country's budget into the army while also paying off debts to the United States. Carías Andino had a friendly relationship with the United Fruit Company and was happy to follow its lead. Finally in 1948, he was forced out of office.

Tiburcio Carías Andino ruled Honduras as a dictator for fifteen years.

Honduras started to see social reform in 1954. Workers at the railroad owned by the United Fruit Company went on strike. They demanded higher wages, improved working conditions, and the ability to join a union. The strike spread to other banana plantations. Soon almost thirty thousand Hondurans had joined the strike. Wages were increased, and trade unions were established for workers.

In 1958, Ramón Villeda Morales of the Liberal Party became president of Honduras. Villeda had many schools, roads, and hospitals built. He also improved laws that helped

Honduran troops head for the front lines during the Soccer War. About two thousand people were killed during the brief war. Most were Honduran civilians.

workers. In October 1963, Honduran military officers overthrew Villeda. He and other Liberal Party members were exiled from Honduras. Colonel Oswaldo López Arellano took control of the country.

While López Arellano was in power in 1969, Honduras went to war with El Salvador. Tensions had been rising because Hondurans were expelling poor Salvadorans who had settled in Honduras without permission. This war became known as the Soccer War. It lasted just two weeks, but during that time, commerce practically came to a halt between the two countries.

In 1975, the army ousted Colonel López Arellano. He was charged with receiving huge bribes from the American fruit company United Brands.

Finally in 1981, democratic elections were held. A civilian president and a legislature were elected by the people. Democratic elections have continued in Honduras up to today.

Military Aid and the United States

During the 1980s, Honduras found itself caught up in the struggle between some of its Central American neighbors and the United States. At the time, the United States was locked in a power struggle with the Soviet Union (which has since split up into Russia and several other eastern European and central Asian nations). U.S. president Ronald Reagan believed that the Nicaraguan government was taking orders from the Soviet Union. To destabilize the government, the United States funded a small army of Nicaraguans, called contras, to fight the Nicaraguan government. The United States was also supplying arms to El Salvador's army to help it fight rebels.

In the 1980s, thousands of Nicaraguan contras trained at camps in Honduras.

Honduras was sandwiched between these two conflicts, and the United States took advantage of its useful location. The United States bribed Honduran military leaders with huge sums of military aid. Airfields and U.S. military bases soon sprang up across Honduras. U.S. troops were stationed there. Americans also gave military training to the Nicaraguan contras and El Salvadoran soldiers.

Some Hondurans were happy to have international attention. Others were concerned that Honduras would be drawn into constant battles. In 1988, the United States withdrew some forces from Honduras, but it still maintains a huge military base outside Comayagua.

Economic Troubles

In the 1990s, Honduras was deeply in debt, owing several billion dollars in international loans. But after Hurricane Mitch in 1998—which destroyed 80 percent of the banana plantations and took out roads, bridges, schools, and hospitals—Honduras attracted international aid. Billions of dollars were donated, and some debts to international lenders were forgiven.

Even though Honduras continued to receive large amounts of aid from other countries, sometimes the money was not distributed correctly. In August 2002, coffee growers demonstrated in Tegucigalpa. They protested against the government

High school teachers went out on strike for two months in 2002 to protest their low wages.

because the coffee growers had not received their share of a $20 million loan from Taiwan to help stimulate the coffee sector. The demonstration became violent, and five hundred protesters were arrested.

That same year, teachers held a strike to protest their low wages and horrible working conditions. Instead of listening to the teachers' demands, the minister of public education reduced the strikers' wages even more.

Ricardo Maduro was elected president on the promise that he would cut crime, but his efforts had little success.

Moving into the Modern World

Honduras still has many problems that need to be addressed. Even so, slowly but surely the country is improving. In 2002, the nation's sixth democratically elected president, Ricardo Maduro, was sworn in. Maduro, a conservative businessman, swore to crack down on crime, attack poverty, and increase government efficiency. His resolve to fight crime is personal: His only son was kidnapped and killed by gang members in 1997. As president, Maduro outlawed all street gangs and announced a zero-tolerance policy regarding their violence. Since then, hundreds of gang members have fled the country.

The memory of Honduras's turbulent times is starting to fade. Instead, law and order has become more common. With that comes the hope of less poverty, better education, and a stable future for the people of Honduras.

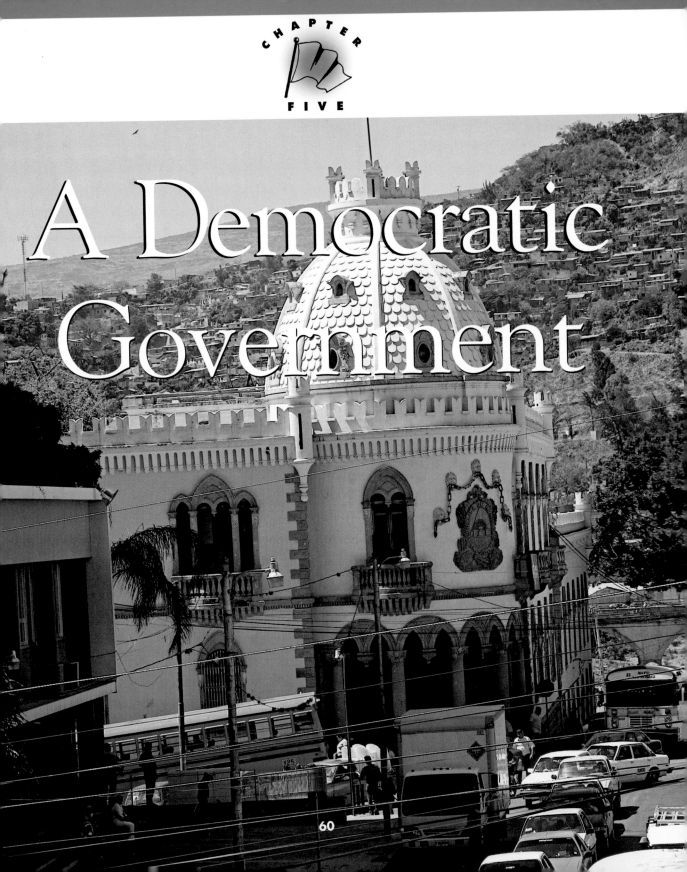

A Democratic Government

HONDURAN HISTORY HAS BEEN FILLED WITH TUMUL-
tuous and often bloody changes in government. But since
1982, it has had democratically elected leaders. The government of Honduras has three branches: executive, legislative,
and judicial.

Opposite: **The Old
Presidential Palace in
Tegucigalpa is now a
museum dedicated to the
history of Honduras starting
from its independence
from Spain.**

Executive Branch

The president is the head of the executive branch and is
elected to a four-year term. A candidate for president must be
Honduran by birth and a current citizen over the age of thirty.
The president may not be reelected.

**Ricardo Maduro served
as president from 2002
until 2006.**

The president has many responsibilities, including ensuring that the constitution and Honduran laws are followed. He or she also names many high-ranking officials. The president appoints a cabinet, which helps with the day-to-day governing of the country. The cabinet is composed of ministers who oversee different sectors of the government. These ministers include the minister of industry and commerce; the minister of finance; and the minister of culture, art, and sports.

Legislative Branch

The legislative branch is made up of one group, called the National Congress. Each of its 128 deputies is elected by the people for a four-year term. All deputies in the National Congress are obliged to vote on any measure presented. The National Congress has the power to approve or disapprove of any actions taken by the executive branch. Its deputies also

The 128 members of the legislative branch meet in the Hall of the National Congress in Tegucigalpa.

To be elected to the Supreme Court, a person must have been a judge for five years or more, be at least thirty-five years old, and be a Honduran by birth.

have the power to declare war, make or change laws, and grant pardons to political prisoners.

Judicial Branch

The judicial branch is made up of several different layers. At the top is the Supreme Court of Justice, which has seven judges and seven substitute judges. They are elected by the National Congress for four-year terms. The Supreme Court can rule on whether any law violates the Honduran constitution. Below the Supreme Court are five Courts of Appeal. These courts can review the actions of the Department Courts, where most trials are held.

NATIONAL GOVERNMENT OF HONDURAS

Executive Branch

PRESIDENT

VICE PRESIDENT

CABINET

Legislative Branch

NATIONAL CONGRESS
(128 DEPUTIES)

Judicial Branch

SUPREME COURT

COURTS OF APPEAL

DEPARTMENT COURTS

National Flag of Honduras

The flag of Honduras came into use on February 16, 1886. It has three horizontal stripes. The upper and lower stripes are blue, and the middle stripe is white. Five blue stars are in the middle of the white stripe, arranged in an X pattern. The stars represent Costa Rica, El Salvador, Guatemala, Honduras, and Nicaragua, the members of the former United Provinces of Central America.

The Constitution

Honduras adopted its current constitution on January 20, 1982. It was amended in 1995. The constitution defines the power of the three branches of government. It also states that any political party that is not democratic shall be banned. In addition, it bans the death penalty, establishes the right to free speech, and defines labor laws, among other issues.

Local Government

Honduras is divided into eighteen departments, or provinces. Each department is headed by a governor, who is appointed by the executive branch of the national government.

The departments are broken down further into cities and towns. Each city is run by a mayor with a council. Mayors make local economic or administrative decisions.

Political Parties and Elections

In Honduras, every adult is required to vote in elections. This rule is not enforced, however.

Throughout its history, Honduras has had two main political parties: The Liberal Party (PL) and the National Party (PN). Today, there are additional parties as well, including the Innovation and Unity Party (PINU), the Christian Democratic Party (PDCH), and the Democratic Unification Party (PUD).

To ensure the elections are held in a fair and correct manner, the National Elections Tribunal keeps watch. The tribunal is an independent division of the government that is responsible for organizing and conducting elections.

Hondurans are eligible to vote when they are eighteen years old. Not only that, but they are required to vote.

Candidates campaign using every means possible. They advertise on television, in the newspapers and on buses. Some people attach

Getting Mail

The postal service of Honduras is run by a private company rather than the government. Most rural houses do not have a mailbox or an address. To send mail, a person living in a rural area has to go to the closest town with a post office. Letters sent to someone in a rural area simply list the person's name and town. For example, the address might read "Max Elvir in La Campa."

loudspeakers to their cars and drive through the streets shouting praises for their candidate. Posters are put up everywhere. They are pasted on houses, cars, and government buildings. Polling stations are set up in the public schools. Because of this, schools may be closed for up to three days prior to elections to get ready.

A sea of red hats greets Liberal Party candidate Roberto Flores at a rally.

The Military

Throughout Honduran history, the military has had a strong political influence. It long operated without any restraints from the government. This changed in 1994, when the government took steps to bring the military under civilian control. It wasn't until 1999, however, that a civilian defense minister was appointed over the military. Honduras has an army, a navy, and an air force. All members of the military are volunteers. In 2003, the army had 8,300 men, the navy had 1,400, and the air force had 2,300.

National Anthem of Honduras

Honduras's national anthem was adopted in 1915. The words are by Augusto C. Coello and the music is by Carlos Hartling.

CHORUS:

Your flag is a splendor of sky
Crossed with a band of snow;
And there can be seen, in its sacred depths,

Five pale blue stars.
In your emblem, which a rough sea
With its wild waves protects,
Behind the bare summit of a volcano,
A star brightly shines.

Like an Indian maiden you were sleeping,
Lulled by the resonant song of your seas,
When, set in your golden valleys,
The bold navigator found you;

And on seeing, enraptured, your beauty,
And feeling your enchantment,
He dedicated a kiss of love to the blue hem
Of your splendid mantle.

To guard this sacred emblem
We shall march, oh fatherland, to our death;
Our death will be honored
If we die thinking of your love.
Having defended your holy flag,
And shrouded in its glorious folds,
Many, Honduras, shall die for you,
But all shall fall in honor.

Tegucigalpa: Did You Know This?

Tegucigalpa, the capital of Honduras, had an estimated population of 850,848 in 2005. Because of its long name, locals often refer to the capital as Tegus. Tegucigalpa is the largest city in Honduras. Historians argue as to whether the name means "silver mountain," because of the silver found in the surrounding mountains, or "place of the painted rocks," because of the pink stone found in the area.

Tegucigalpa is nestled in a valley in the mountains of south-central Honduras, next to the Choluteca River.

The city is rich in history. The Spanish founded it in 1578 as a center for silver and gold mining. The oldest part of the city is located on the slopes of Mount Picacho. In this area, narrow brick and stone streets meander up hills.

Downtown is the National Cathedral and the old Presidential Palace, which now houses a museum of Honduran history. Many banks, hotels, and office buildings surround Central Park. Though Tegucigalpa is a modern city, it is one of the few capitals in the world that does not have a railroad.

Slums cover many of the hillsides surrounding Tegucigalpa. Most of these slums do not have running water. Instead, water must be bought from a water truck.

Comayagüela, a city south of the Choluteca River, became a part of Tegucigalpa in 1938. Today, some parts of Comayagüela are dangerous because of gangs and gang-related crime.

When Hurricane Mitch struck Honduras in 1998, Tegucigalpa suffered significant damage. Mudslides devastated entire neighborhoods built on the mountainous slopes. These areas have not been rebuilt.

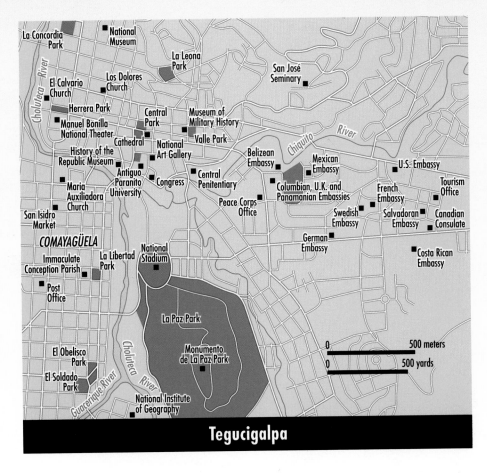

Tegucigalpa

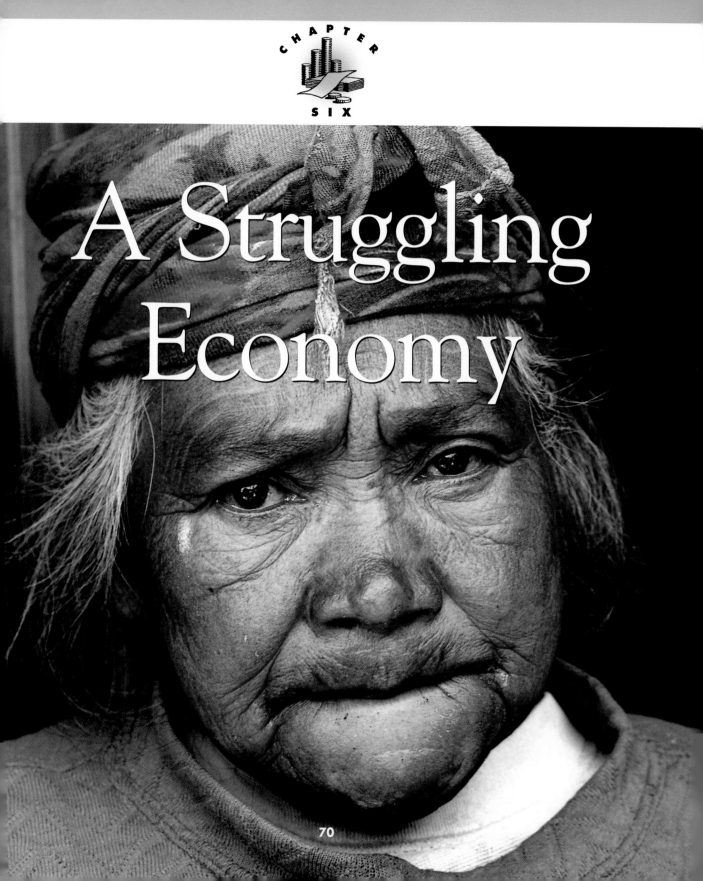

A Struggling Economy

HONDURAS IS ONE OF THE POOREST NATIONS IN THE Western Hemisphere. Almost 80 percent of all Hondurans live in poverty.

More than half of working Hondurans are self-employed. They might be craftspeople, shopkeepers, or subsistence farmers whose farms only produce enough to feed themselves. The self-employed may earn extra money by working on a plantation for part of the year. Some women in the cities work as street vendors selling goods or as domestic help in middle- and upper-class Honduran families. The minimum wage in Honduras in 2004 was $1.09 per hour. Unemployment is very high. In 2003, about 28 percent of Hondurans were unemployed.

Opposite: **Almost half of Hondurans live in extreme poverty.**

A woman sells vegetables on the streets of Tegucigalpa.

Money Facts

The Honduran lempira is Honduras's basic unit of currency. It is named after the Lenca chief who fought against the Spanish in the sixteenth century. Lempira banknotes show pictures of leaders from Honduran history or cultural sites. For example, the 1-lempira note shows a portrait of Lempira on one side and a ball court in the Copán ruins on the other.

One lempira is divided into 100 centavos. The coins are worth 5, 10, 20, and 50 centavos. In the past, there were also 1- and 2-centavo coins, but these are being phased out. Lempira banknotes come in values of 1, 2, 5, 10, 20, 50, 100, and 500. In 2006, about 19 lempiras equaled 1 U.S. dollar.

The Honduran Economy

Honduras produced approximately $17.55 billion worth of goods and services in the year 2003. Services, such as tourism, insurance, and real estate, contributed the greatest portion of this total, an estimated 55 percent. Industry, which includes mining, manufacturing, construction, and power, contributed about 32 percent. Agriculture, which includes farming, fishing, forestry, and hunting, contributed an estimated 13 percent.

Manufacturing

Honduras has one of the least developed economies in Latin America. The main industries are sugar, coffee, textiles, clothing, and wood products. San Pedro Sula is the main manufacturing center in Honduras. Some manufacturing also takes place in Tegucigalpa. In both of these cities, textiles, cigarettes, detergents, foods, beverages, and clothing are manufactured. In addition, sawmills cut lumber, which is then made into furniture or paper.

Pottery is also manufactured in Honduras. But rather than being made in factories, pottery is handcrafted by Hondurans in their homes and then sold in local shops.

Honduras exports more clothes to the United States than any country except China and Mexico.

The main crops in Honduras are bananas, coffee, corn, and citrus fruit. Honduras's mountainous landscape makes farming difficult. Only 15 percent of the country's land can be used for farming.

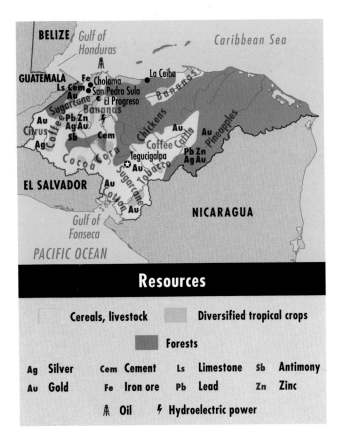

The majority of income received by Honduras from other countries is from its export of shellfish, bananas, and coffee. Livestock is another important part of the economy. In 2002, Hondurans raised 19,000,000 chickens, 1,730,000 cows, 480,000 pigs, 32,000 goats, and 14,000 sheep.

Honduras has many different mineral resources. They include gold, silver, copper, lead, zinc, coal, iron ore, and antimony, a metal used to harden metals that have been combined. Timber is also an important resource in Honduras.

Honduras uses hydroelectric power for much of its electricity. Hydroelectric power is produced by damming a river and routing the water through a turbine. In 2000, this type of power accounted for 62 percent of all electricity in Honduras. The remaining 38 percent was provided by petroleum. Honduras has long lacked a consistent power source, so power shortages often result. In La Ceiba and

San Pedro Sula, power blackouts sometimes occur three times a day. Tegucigalpa residents expect a blackout at least once a day on Sundays.

Poor rural Hondurans do not rely on electricity. Instead, they use wood to cook their food and heat their homes.

A man carries a bucket of coffee beans. Honduras is home to thousands of small coffee farms.

Weights and Measures

Honduras's system of weights and measures is a combination of the metric system and an old Spanish-pound system called libras. For example, 25 libras equal 25 pounds (11 kg) as well as 1 arroba. Four arrobas equal 100 pounds (45 kg) and 1 quintal.

Even though some items are still measured in quarts and gallons, such as milk, Honduras is trying to completely convert to the metric system of liters.

Distance is measured in meters. For example, 1 kilometer equals 0.6 mile.

Imports and Exports

Honduras imports more goods than it exports. Its largest import and export partner is the United States. In 2003, Honduras imported $3.1 billion worth of goods, including machinery, fuel, chemical products, and food. Fifty-three percent of these imports came from the United States. Mexico was second and El Salvador, third.

Bananas are loaded into railroad cars that will be shipped to the United States. It is estimated that the banana industry provides jobs to at least 150,000 Hondurans.

What Honduras Grows, Makes, and Mines

Agriculture (2004)

Sugarcane	5,360,000 metric tons
Bananas/plantains	1,021,215 metric tons
Oil palm fruit	178,000 metric tons

Manufacturing Exports (2003)

Coffee	U.S.$183,300,000
Wood products	U.S.$59,600,000
Palm oil	U.S.$53,900,000

Mining

Silver	53,000 metric tons
Zinc	46,000 metric tons
Lead	8,000 metric tons

Honduras's exports in the same year totaled $1.37 billion. Top exports included coffee, bananas, shrimp, lobster, beef, zinc, and lumber. About 69 percent of these exports went to the United States. Honduras's other leading export partners were El Salvador and Guatemala.

Many factors that influence the Honduran economy are well beyond the country's control. The Honduran economy is intimately connected to the United States because of their trading relationship. If the U.S. economy does poorly, Honduras will be affected. The cost of goods around the world also has a big effect on Honduras. The prices of coffee and bananas are particularly important.

Another economic problem in Honduras is crime, particularly drug crimes. Tegucigalpa alone has about a hundred youth gangs. Honduras also has many outstanding debts to other countries. In 2003, Honduras owed about $5.2 billion.

Transportation

Honduras has few roads, and many of them are not paved, especially in rural areas. In 2002, the nation had only 8,504 miles (13,686 km) of highways. Just 1,773 miles (2,853 km) of them were paved.

Few people own cars in rural areas. Instead, they ride on public buses. These old, yellow school buses are seen throughout the country. Hitchhiking is another widespread form of transportation. It is not uncommon to see more than twenty hitchhikers crammed into the back of a pickup truck. If the

Only seven out of every thousand Hondurans own a car, so many people hitchhike.

Pack animals are often the best way to get around in the jungle.

road gets too rough and the truck stalls, everyone unloads and pushes the truck until it starts again. It is an unwritten law in rural areas that if a car or truck drives by a walking schoolteacher, the driver must stop and give him or her a ride. Another means of transportation in rural areas is mountain bikes, which are called the "new mule."

Real mules and horses are sometimes used to get around in rural areas. Outside San Pedro Sula, horses pulling carts sometimes race along with rush-hour traffic in the morning.

There are only 434 miles (698 km) of railroad track in Honduras. These tracks are in the northern part of the country, where most trains are used to transport fruit.

Honduras has twelve airports with paved runways. The airports in Tegucigalpa, San Pedro Sula, La Ceiba, and Roatán are international airports. Airplanes landing in Tegucigalpa must navigate through steep mountains. Fires dot the slopes

Common Items in a Store in Honduras

½ gallon of milk	22 lempira	U.S.$1.22
1 pound ground beef	35 lempira	U.S.$1.94
15 eggs	26 lempira	U.S.$1.44
1 pound bananas	3 lempira	U.S.$0.17
1 can soda pop	7 lempira	U.S.$0.39
1 loaf of bread	18 lempira	U.S.$0.99
1 candy bar	15 lempira	U.S.$0.83

and smoke fills the air where farmers or squatters are burning plants to clear the land. Sometimes the smoke gets so thick that planes are unable to land. When this happens, flights are diverted to either San Pedro Sula or El Salvador, and then passengers are bused into Tegucigalpa.

The main port in Honduras is Puerto Cortés, on the Caribbean Sea. It is one of the largest ports in all of Central America. Honduras also has six other ports.

Communications

Few Hondurans own television sets or radios. The country averages about one television and four radios for every ten people. Cable television is hugely popular, though. Some people will get cable TV before they have indoor plumbing.

There are seven daily newspapers in Honduras. The largest, called *La Prensa*, is published in San Pedro Sula. Because computers are expensive, few people use the Internet. Internet service providers in Honduras give inconsistent service.

A woman sells newspapers at the bus station in San Pedro Sula.

Even so, Internet cafes are easy to find in most cities and towns of Honduras.

Cell phones are becoming more popular than landline phones. In 2005, there were 400,000 landline phones in use and 1,114,427 cell phones.

Free Zone Law

Honduras is one of several countries that have approved the Free Zone Law. This law allows companies from other countries to set up manufacturing plants in Honduras. The companies can import materials or equipment that are required by their plants without any fee. They are also allowed to export their finished products without any fees. These plants are called *maquilas*. The first maquila in Honduras began operating in 1976. Because of the Free Zone Law, these foreign companies give jobs to local Hondurans. The Honduran government sees little or no financial gain from the exported products.

In 2000, maquilas provided more than 110,000 jobs in Honduras. However, the employees sometimes have to work long hours, receive low pay, and suffer health problems caused by their working conditions.

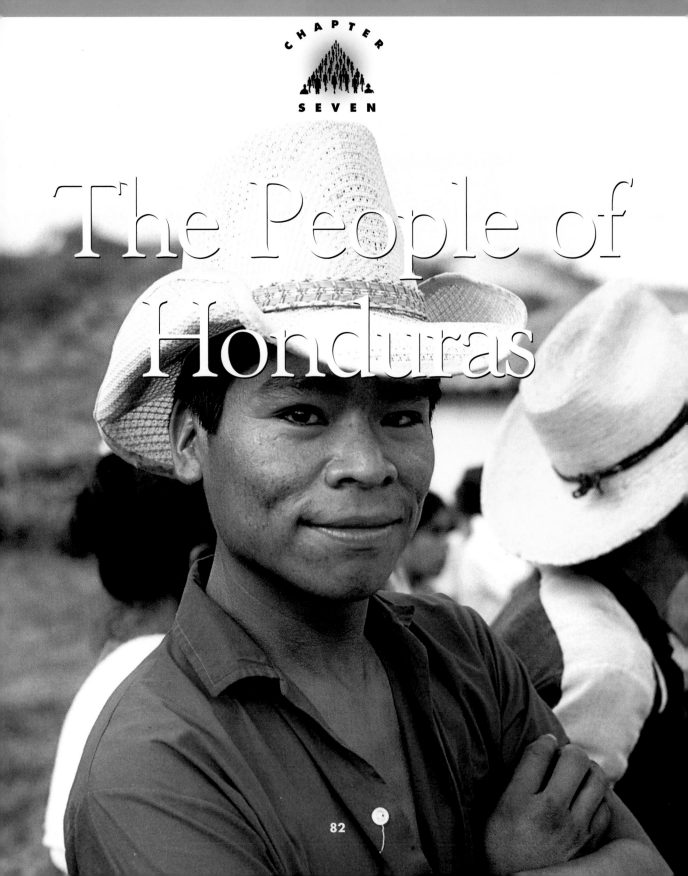

The People of Honduras

Forty-one percent of
Hondurans are less than
fifteen years old.

H ONDURANS TEND TO BE FRIENDLY AND HOSPITABLE
people. They love fiestas and will celebrate any event with
enthusiasm. Family is everything to the people of Honduras.
Members of tight-knit families rely on one another through
good and bad times.

Ethnic Groups

In 2005, an estimated 6,975,204 people lived in Honduras.
About 90 percent of Hondurans are mestizo, people of mixed
European and indigenous descent. Mestizos speak Spanish,
and most belong to the Roman Catholic Church.

Opposite: **Almost half
of Hondurans live in
rural areas.**

Ethnic Honduras

Mestizo	90%
Indigenous	7%
Black	2%
White	1%

About one hundred thousand Lenca live in Honduras. The women are known for their bright dresses.

Honduras is home to several other ethnic groups besides mestizos. The Lenca, who live in the southwestern part of the country, are the largest native group in Honduras. Most are farmers who use digging sticks to plow the land. Both men and women work in the fields. Lenca women wear bright dresses of a single color. They also wear colorful sweaters and bright, multicolored head scarves. The Lenca are skilled at making baskets and pottery.

The Pipil and the Chortí Maya live in the western tip of Honduras. The Pipil, who are the descendants of indigenous tribes from Mexico called the Toltec, live on mountain slopes. The Chortí Maya are descendants of the ancient Maya. They are skilled in making leather and wood products.

Another ethnic group is the Miskito. They live on the Mosquito Coast in northeastern Honduras. The Miskito are a mix of European, African, and indigenous peoples. They speak their own language, which is similar to languages spoken by native groups in South America. The Miskito burn the forest to clear land for farming plots. Once the land no longer yields crops, they move to another area of the forest to start again. The Miskito grow beans, corn, and yucca, and they raise cows, pigs, and chickens. Because the Miskito live in a swampy, watery region, they travel around in dugout canoes and flat-bottom boats. Fishing is important to them as well.

The people of the Mosquito Coast use boats to get around.

Also living on the Mosquito Coast are the Tawahka and the Pech. Both groups fish and farm. They are extremely knowledgeable about how to survive in the forest. The Tawahka migrated to Honduras from Colombia in South America. The Pech were originally from west-central Honduras. During the Spanish conquest, they migrated east to escape the Spanish and find farmland. They cultivate various roots such as yucca for food.

The Tolupán live in the central part of Honduras. They still maintain ancient traditions such as hunting with blowguns. Their homes are made of planks tied with vines.

Fishing is central to the Garifuna lifestyle.

Two ethnic groups of African descent live in Honduras. One is the Garífunas, who are also known as the Black Caribs. They live on the Caribbean coast and parts of the Bay Islands. The Garífunas are descendants of freed African slaves who arrived in Honduras during the second half of the seventeenth century. They have their own language, customs, music, and dances. One traditional Garífuna dance is the punta. Women

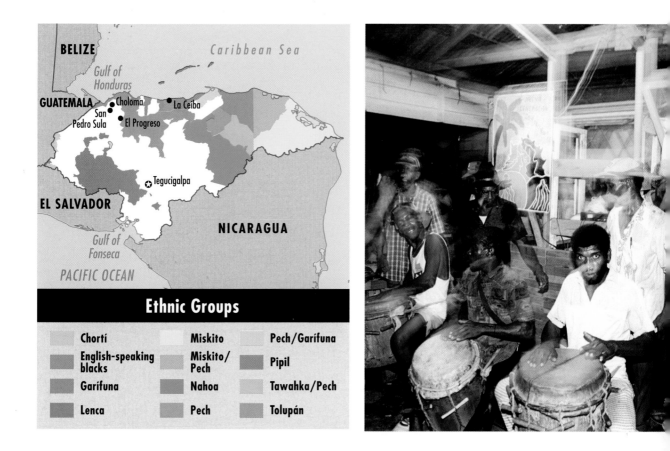

dance the punta to show that they are ready to have children, to show their feelings of joy, and to make other people happy. It also may help them to find a husband. During religious ceremonies, the Garífunas beat drums and sometimes sacrifice animals.

The second ethnic group of African descent also live on the Bay Islands. They are descendants of English-speaking blacks and whites. They speak Caribbean English, and their traditions are similar to those of other English-speaking peoples who live on Caribbean islands.

Punta is probably the most popular Garífuna dance. Its origins date back to the Garífunas' ancestors in West Africa.

Spanish Numbers

uno	one
dos	two
tres	three
cuatro	four
cinco	five
seis	six
siete	seven
ocho	eight
nueve	nine
diez	ten

Honduran Languages

The national language of Honduras is Spanish. In Spanish, there are formal and informal ways of addressing a person. For instance, if you're speaking to a friend, you use one form of a verb. If you're speaking to a stranger, you use a different form of the verb.

In smaller villages, people speak native languages such as Chortí Maya. Garífunas living on the Caribbean coast speak a language called Garifuna, which stems from Arawakan, an indigenous language of South America and the Caribbean. They also speak Spanish and English. English is understood along the Caribbean coast because of the long influence of U.S. fruit companies there. English is also spoken by some people living on the Bay Islands. In northeastern Honduras, the Miskito speak their own language, which is called Miskito.

Common Spanish Words and Phrases

Hola	Hello
Adiós	Good-bye
Buenos días	Good morning
Buenas tardes	Good afternoon
Buenas noches	Good evening
¿Cómo estás?	How are you?
Muy bien	Very well
Gracias	Thank you
De nada	You're welcome
Sí	Yes
No	No
Perdóneme	Excuse me
Por favor	Please

Most Hondurans dress casually. Men wear comfortable loose pants and shirts. Women wear cotton dresses or loose blouses and skirts. Sandals are common because the weather is often hot and humid. Most poor Hondurans have to wear second-hand clothing.

During fiestas, Hondurans wear their best clothing and elaborate costumes. To celebrate the festivities, women sometimes wear special dresses of silk or cotton embroidered in Mayan designs.

Cowboy hats are popular among Honduran men. The hat's wide brim protects the face from the burning sun.

Population of Honduras's Largest Cities (2005 estimate)	
Tegucigalpa	850,848
San Pedro Sula	489,466
Choloma	139,800
La Ceiba	130,218
El Progreso	100,810
Choluteca	75,872

In the cities, how people dress depends on their jobs. Some Hondurans wear suits or nice skirts and blouses. Others dress more casually in jeans with nice shirts. Women in business wear high heels, whereas street vendors wear flat shoes.

In the country, women wear skirts and blouses with flat shoes or sandals, and men wear jeans or casual pants with T-shirts or buttoned shirts. Cowboy hats are common, to shade workers from the hot sun. Honduran men and women never wear shorts.

Education

Honduras did not have a nationwide school system until the 1950s. In 1998, about a quarter of Hondurans could not read or write. On average, a twenty-five-year-old Honduran had gone to school for just five years. These numbers were among the lowest in Central America.

Today, Honduran children between the ages of seven and twelve are required to go to school. The government provides this education for free. In 2000, 88 percent of children between these ages were in school. But only about 35 percent of them continued on to secondary school.

All students must wear a school uniform of a white shirt and blue pants or skirt. In some schools, the rule is loosely followed and some students wear blue jeans.

Rural schools sometimes have several grades in one room. For example, third, fourth, and fifth graders may all be in one room. The teacher might give a short lecture to the third and fourth graders. Then she will give those students an

assignment. While they are working on it, she will lecture the fifth graders and then give them an assignment. She does this all day long, switching back and forth among the different grades in her room. Rural schools are often informal, too. Dogs may wander in and out of the classrooms.

Depending on the school, the children might have textbooks. In the fifth grade, Honduran children learn about North, Central, and South American geography and history, Spanish grammar, and beginning geometry. Some Honduran schools also have a program called Values of Honduras. Different values are focused on each month. For instance, February values are family, self-esteem, and self-awareness. March values are respect of self and others. These values are posted and then stressed for that month in the school.

All students in Honduras must wear uniforms.

Students continuing in school past age twelve go to secondary schools. Secondary education has two stages. The first stage is grades seven through nine when general topics are studied. The second stage is a two-year program. In this stage, students study specific topics that are geared to the career they're interested in, such as teaching, carpentry, and computer technology. Only those students completing both stages of secondary education are considered for a university.

Honduras has many private schools. These schools charge a fee, so they are only available to the middle and upper classes. Many are Catholic or Protestant boarding schools. Some large foreign corporations have established schools for their employees' children.

There are seven universities in Honduras. The oldest and largest is the National Autonomous University of Honduras. It is located in Tegucigalpa and has branches in San Pedro Sula and La Ceiba. The school was founded by Father José Trinidad Reyes in 1847.

Throughout the years, the Honduran government has increased spending on education. In 2003, the educational budget was 8,783,000 lempira ($462,000), which was 27 percent of the total government budget. Even so, there is still a shortage of schools, teachers, and textbooks. Some classes have as many as fifty students. This shortage of funds came to international attention, and in 2000 and 2003, Honduras received about $120 million in financial aid from the Inter-American Development Bank and the World Bank. This aid was to assist the Honduran government in reforming its educational system and allowing more children to attend secondary school.

Rural Hondurans

Most Hondurans living in the countryside are poor farmers called campesinos. They use machetes and plows sometimes drawn by oxen. To clear the land, the campesinos cut and burn away the natural vegetation. After using the land for a few years, they move on to new land because the soil no longer produces crops.

Some campesinos own or rent their small farm. Often they are isolated and don't know what is happening in the cities.

Oxen are popular among rural Hondurans. The animals are strong, gentle, and hardworking, yet easy to care for.

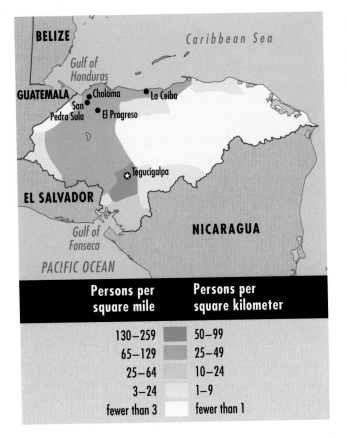

Persons per square mile	Persons per square kilometer
130–259	50–99
65–129	25–49
25–64	10–24
3–24	1–9
fewer than 3	fewer than 1

Transportation and communication is extremely poor. Changes in the cities of Honduras sometimes take months or years to reach rural Honduras.

Urban Hondurans

Honduran cities are home to people of all backgrounds. Upper-class Hondurans include people who own large farms or ranches and top financial and military leaders. The upper class controls political power and medical care. They also have the greatest educational opportunities. For many years, Honduras did not have a middle class. But the rise of government jobs and mid-level jobs in industry and commerce have led to the growth of a middle class. Poor Hondurans who live in cities have jobs such as nanny, house cleaner, or assembly-line worker.

Honduras has fewer social tensions between the upper and lower classes than other Central American countries. One reason for this is that Honduras has a large number of poor, rural farmers who work their own land. In other countries, rural farmers usually work land belonging to someone else. Hondurans generally believe in equal rights for all citizens, rich or poor.

Health Care Issues

Providing good health care to all Hondurans has been a constant problem. The average male Honduran can expect to live about sixty-four years and the average female about seventy. Infant mortality is high, with about thirty out of every one thousand babies dying before their first birthday. About one-third of all young Honduran children are malnourished, meaning they do not get enough food or vitamins and minerals to be healthy. Nor are there enough medical facilities for all Hondurans. Deadly diseases such as malaria, typhoid, tuberculosis, and pneumonia are common. A lack of clean drinking water makes Hondurans' health problems even worse.

Children in cities often suffer from respiratory illnesses due to poor air quality. However, residents in urban areas have greater access to medical care than those in rural Honduras.

Spiritual Life

M ost Hondurans are Roman Catholic. Catholicism was introduced to Honduras by the Spanish hundreds of years ago. When the Spanish first arrived in Honduras, the indigenous people held ceremonies that dated back to the time of the ancient Maya. Some of these ceremonies are still practiced today.

Opposite: **Honduras is filled with shrines depicting the baby Jesus and his mother.**

Honduras's religious statues are often quite colorful.

The Catholic Religion

The rituals and traditions of Catholicism are a basic part of Honduran society. Catholic churches can be found in almost every village, pueblo, or city. In the village of San Manuel Colohete is a church built in the seventeenth century. The village, located far up in the mountains in western Honduras, is accessible only by dirt road. The church's ornate facade is white, with pastel-colored statues in alcoves.

Saints are a very important part of Catholicism. In colonial times, the tradition of a saint's feast was started. The Spanish dedicated each town or village to a special patron saint. The city of Tegucigalpa was dedicated to

The Virgin of Suyapa

Honduras's patron saint is the Virgin of Suyapa. This is a tiny statue of the Virgin Mary, Jesus's mother, that stands just 2.6 inches (6.5 cm) tall. Mary wears a rose-colored dress and a blue cape. Both are trimmed in gold and silver with many precious stones. According to legend, the painted wood statue was found in a cornfield. Today, it is housed in the Church of Suyapa. This beautiful white church was built in the eighteenth century by the Spanish.

Many worshippers visit the Church of Suyapa to pray to the statue. It is said that she will grant a person's wish if they ask with a pure heart. Through the years, Hondurans have given the Virgin of Suyapa credit for many great events. She has been credited with helping Honduras beat El Salvador in the Soccer War. She has even been named High Captain of the Armed Forces by the Honduran army.

In early February, there is a weeklong festival celebrating the Virgin of Suyapa. Masses, concerts, canon salutes, and a midnight fireworks display are all part of the celebration. Pilgrims come from as far north as Mexico and as far south as Colombia to pray to the virgin. Because the virgin attracts so many visitors, a large shrine was built in front of the older chapel. Pope John Paul II visited this new shrine in 1983.

Saint Michael. One day out of the year is set aside for the saint's feast. Many Hondurans have pictures or statues of a saint in their homes. They pray to the saint, asking for help or assistance. Making pilgrimages to sacred shrines dedicated to saints is also common.

Children dressed as angels wait for the start of an event honoring St. Michael, Tegucigalpa's patron saint.

Other Christian Religions

Besides Catholicism, more than three hundred other Christian faiths are practiced in Honduras. Churches include the Episcopal Church, the Lutheran Church, Jehovah's Witnesses, the Church of Jesus Christ of Latter-day Saints (Mormons), Abundant Life, and Living Love.

Religions of Honduras

Roman Catholic	63%
Evangelical Protestant	23%
Other or none	14%

A masked man leads villagers in a guancasco celebration at La Campa.

Ancient Rituals

Indigenous Hondurans have long mixed ancient native traditions with Catholic ceremonies. After the Lenca converted to Catholicism, they continued to pray to their ancient gods as well as to the new one. To the Lenca, any religious object or person was valid. In the Mayan culture, the ceiba tree was

Death Ceremonies

When someone dies, Catholics in Honduras pray for nine evenings, usually at home but sometimes in the local church. A special altar is made that has candles and flowers. On the ninth day, they pray all day until midnight. They also drink coffee and eat bread and tamales (steamed cornmeal filled with meat or beans and wrapped in a corn husk). The next morning, they take the flowers from the altar down to the cemetery. This ritual is called the novena. It is repeated one year later. The Garífunas perform this ritual slightly differently. They do not believe the soul of a person is ready to go to the land of ancestors right after death. Instead, they believe it takes a year for a soul to prepare. To point the soul in the right direction, a ceremony is performed in which a doll representing the dead person is placed in the sea.

the tree of life. Today, it is very common to find a ceiba tree planted next to a Catholic church.

Another Lenca tradition is called *guancasco*. This is a ceremony of peace between two neighboring villages to show continued assistance and friendship. It is celebrated on a village's patron saint's day.

A guancasco is held almost every year in the village of La Campa, which is located in a valley surrounded by sheer rocky cliffs. Vendors flood the tiny village to sell bales of garlic, watches, candy, agave nets, bundles of chamomile, and clothing. The ceremony starts when firecrackers explode. The church bell rings, and a man emerges from the church wearing a mask. In one hand is a stuffed iguana and in the other, a whip. A drum starts to beat as a flute is played. The masked man walks up the hill to the next village. Following behind him is a statue of the saint of the church balanced on shoulders and a long line of faithful believers. The ceremony ends once the saint of La Campa has been exchanged with a neighboring village's saint.

The Chortí Maya often burn a hardened sap called copal while they pray and while performing a ritual to help a sick person. Copal is used to rid the air of bad spirits and as a symbol for the clouds.

To native Hondurans, the Virgin Mary also represents the indigenous goddess of fertility, healing, and medicine. The sun is very important to them because it brings energy inside people, plants, and animals. A good harvest depends on the sun. Christ is sometimes represented as the sun, and the Virgin Mary is represented as the moon.

Important Honduran Religious Holidays

January 6
Feast of the Three Kings, the day when the Three Wise Men are supposed to have visited the baby Jesus. In Honduras, it is traditional to exchange gifts on this day.

February 2
The feast day of the Virgin of Suyapa, Honduras's patron saint. The climax of this celebration features her image balanced on shoulders with a long procession following.

Late March or early April
Holy Week and Easter, which are extremely important to Hondurans. In several cities, this four-day holiday is filled with religious processions of enactments of Bible stories. In addition, elaborate, colorful carpets made of sawdust are created on the streets.

December 16–24
Las Posadas ("the lodgings"). Each night during this time, there is a celebration commemorating the story of Joseph and Mary looking for lodging before she gives birth. Couples enact the Bible story by searching for lodging. Bible reading, religious meditation, and food are also part of the celebration.

December 25
Christmas Day, when many people put out statues depicting the baby Jesus in the manger.

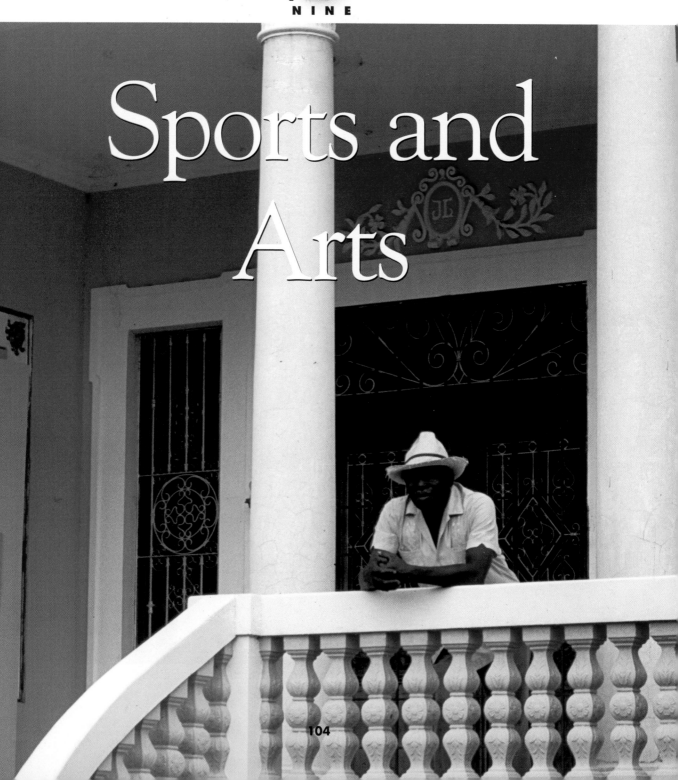

Sports and Arts

H

ONDURANS HAVE A RICH AND VARIED CULTURAL
heritage. They also love to play sports, especially their favorite, soccer.

Opposite: **A man leans on a railing at the National Museum in Tegucigalpa.**

The National Sport

In Honduras, *fútbol*, or soccer, is the national sport. National
games are played in two main stadiums. One is the Tiburcio
Carías Andino National Stadium in Tegucigalpa, and the other
is General Francisco Morazán Stadium in San Pedro Sula.

The Honduran national soccer team draws huge crowds whenever it plays.

Hondurans are passionate about soccer. They dress up in their team colors while attending the games. If a big soccer game is being played in town, it's as if the whole place shuts down. Everyone is either at the game or listening to it on the radio. Because soccer is so popular, just about every town in Honduras has an organized soccer team. Soccer is played almost every Sunday afternoon, even when it is extremely hot outside. In addition, banana plantation or construction workers may find time to play a game of soccer during their lunch hour. After a crop is harvested in a rural area, the field may be used for playing soccer.

Soccer is by far the most popular sport in Honduras. People will play wherever they can find an open space.

The Soccer War

Tensions were running high between El Salvador and Honduras in the 1960s. One reason was that thousands of Salvadorans had crossed the border into Honduras and settled there illegally. This took land, jobs, and farms away from Hondurans. In 1969, the Honduran government gave the illegal immigrants an ultimatum to leave Honduras. By late May that year, thousands began to stream back into El Salvador.

In 1969, the teams of Honduras and El Salvador were playing each other in a qualifying match for the World Cup, the championship of soccer. They were scheduled for a three-game elimination match. Their first game was held in Tegucigalpa. Rivalry ran high as El Salvador lost the first game. Later that month, the Honduran team went to El Salvador to play the second game. During the game, some people insulted the Honduran flag and national anthem. Several visiting Hondurans were injured. Honduras lost the game. Because of the violence, the third game was postponed.

One month later, on July 14, the Salvadoran army invaded Honduras. It progressed deep into the country, but its advance was brought to a halt when the Honduran army destroyed El Salvador's fuel supply. The war lasted only one hundred hours.

Tourism is on the rise in Honduras. Kayaking is popular among visitors to the Bay Islands.

Other Honduran Sports

Students at some private schools play basketball, baseball, and tennis. In Honduras's larger cities, wealthy businessmen regularly play golf. Pool halls are set up in some villages, but only men are allowed to play.

The Bay Islands are filled with sporting opportunities. Wealthy Hondurans fish for sailfish, kingfish, red snapper, and shark. Tourists arrive to go scuba diving, snorkeling, and horseback riding.

Dancing is another popular activity. Folk dancing is very common during fiestas. More than twenty different folk dances are common in Honduras. Some of these dances have Spanish roots. Others can be traced back to their indigenous or African origins. Social dancing is also common. Many people dance to salsa and Mexican ranchero music.

White clothes with rainbow stripes are typical for folk dancers of the Intibucá region of western Honduras.

The National Art Gallery

The National Art Gallery is housed in a restored colonial building close to the Central Park of Tegucigalpa. This gallery shows the evolution of artwork in Honduras. It starts with cave art, Mayan pottery, and ornate religious pieces made of silver.

The top floor showcases modern Honduran artists such as Pablo Zelaya Sierra, the father of the Honduran modern art movement, and José Antonio Velásquez, who is known for his primitive-style paintings of rural Honduras.

José Antonio Velásquez was one of the most popular Honduran painters of the 1960s and 1970s. His paintings are known for their warm depictions of villages.

Honduran Writers and Painters

One of the first and most important writers from Honduras is Father José Trinidad Reyes, who lived from 1797 to 1855. This Catholic priest wrote poems and plays. He also founded the first university in Honduras. Another famous Honduran is Juan Ramón Molina, a nineteenth-century poet. His poems were published in magazines and newspapers throughout Central America. Later, his best poems were compiled and published in a book titled *Seas and Skies*. In the twentieth century, Rafael Heliodoro Valle, a poet and historian, was highly respected throughout the world.

Several Honduran painters made international names for themselves in the twentieth century. Arturo López Rodezno founded the School of Fine Arts. Both Carlos Garay and José Antonio Velásquez became known for their landscape paintings.

The School of Fine Arts in Comayagüela

The School of Fine Arts is located across the Choluteca River from Tegucigalpa in its twin city, Comayagüela. The school is paid for by the government. Students receive a free education, though they must pay for their own materials. Only those with the most artistic skill are accepted into the school.

Students attend the school for up to three years. During this time, they have four academic classes per day. These classes include math, science, social studies, and Spanish. In addition, they have four art classes per day. Some of the arts taught at this school are restoration, sculpture, painting, ceramics, pottery, graphics, silk screening, photography, and drawing. Once the students graduate, they can continue on to college. Some graduates of this school have become famous artists in Honduras and abroad.

Folk Art

Hondurans are skilled at making art objects such as wooden furniture, baskets, mats, and wall hangings. Brightly colored ceramics are formed into vases and hollowed-out animals. Beautiful, distinctive pottery is made by the Lenca tribe. Leather goods are cut into belts and handbags. Hand-stitched embroidery is sewn onto blouses and dresses. Silver is shaped into unusual jewelry. Near Copán, marble carvings shaped into replicas of the ruins can be found.

Designs such as birds and insects brighten Honduran cloth.

An Artist for the Lenca

Up-and-coming artist Eduardo Galeano was born in Gracias in 1966. While growing up, he would listen to tales of the Lenca from his Lenca gardener. Galeano absorbed these tales, and they became part of him. After graduating from the School of Fine Arts, he began painting. He used oil, watercolor, charcoal, pencil, and pastel chalk—all on the same theme, the Lenca. Each of his paintings and drawings portrays Lenca history, buildings, and symbols. Galeano's art has been shown in Honduras, the United States, Germany, and Spain.

Opposite: **An audience enjoys the show at the Manuel Bonilla National Theater. The theater hosts everything from the National Symphonic Orchestra to a telethon for disabled children.**

Theater

The two largest theaters in Honduras are in Tegucigalpa and San Pedro Sula. The Manuel Bonilla National Theater in Tegucigalpa was built in 1915. The beautiful, ornate interior seats six hundred people. The theater is used for orchestra performances, European plays, dance performances, and special presentations for visiting foreign dignitaries.

Traditional Honduran musical instruments were made from material easy to find in the local environment. Some of these were drums made of animal skin, trumpets constructed of bamboo or wood, and whistles and flutes formed from clay.

The Garífunas turned conch shells into horns, tortoise shells into drums, and gourds into maracas. When the Spanish arrived, they introduced guitars and other stringed instruments to Honduras.

Drums play a central role in Garífuna ceremonies. Following a death, drums are used to summon the spirits of those who have died before.

A Honduran International Musician

Guillermo Anderson, a native of La Ceiba, entered the Honduran music scene playing his acoustic guitar accompanied by two Garífuna drummers. He gained instant recognition. He was approached by the Honduran Ministry of Culture and asked to represent Honduras in festivals and concerts throughout the world.

At home in Honduras, his popularity exploded when the video of his song "En Mi País" ("In My Country") was aired on Honduran television at the close of its programming. Many children love Anderson's music. His song "Fiesta en el Bosque" ("Party in the Forest") was written for children and is in high demand.

Anderson toured Europe with an eight-piece band called Ceibana to raise money for the victims of Hurricane Mitch in 1998. Ceibana includes a rhythmic dancer along with a full percussion section. Anderson's music is influenced by reggae and salsa along with jazz and rock.

Living in Honduras

BECAUSE THE LANDSCAPES OF HONDURAS VARY SO WIDELY, there are many different types of lifestyles. The cities are polluted and hectic, whereas the country is dusty and slow. On the islands, life is ruled by the crashing waves of the Caribbean Sea.

Opposite: **More than 90 percent of Hondurans are mestizo. They have both Spanish and indigenous ancestors.**

Housing

In rural Honduras, many homes are made of adobe (dried mud-bricks) with a tiled roof. Inside are two rooms. Poorer people make their homes out of whatever they can find. They might live in houses made of bamboo, sugarcane, and cornstalks. Some houses are made of dirt and stones wedged between rickety wooden frames. Some are even constructed out of cardboard, trash bags, or scraps of plastic.

In the mountains of Honduras, most people live in simple adobe houses with tile roofs.

Making Adobe

Adobe is made from mud or horse manure mixed with pine needles, straw, or grass to make it firm. This mixture is placed in a wooden frame about 2 feet (0.6 m) long, 1 foot (0.3 m) wide, and 6 inches (15 cm) thick. After the mixture is smoothed, the frame is removed. The bricks are left in the sun for three days to dry.

In the country, beds can be hammocks or mats on the floor. Tree stumps may serve as chairs. The poor rarely have running water or electricity. They collect water from nearby streams and carry it home by cow or mule. During the rainy season, water drums are put out to collect the rain. Wood is burned to cook and to heat the home. Because of this, the smell of burning wood permeates the air.

Most homes in Honduras do not have running water, so people must collect water and carry it home.

Adobe homes usually do not have glass windows. Instead, the windows are open during the day. At night, wooden shutters cover the window openings.

The upper and middle classes live in houses made of thick brick, concrete, or adobe. Sometimes these houses have two stories. Strong metal window grills protect the homes from thieves. Many wealthy Hondurans hire servants to help them around the house.

Some wealthy Hondurans live in large homes protected by fences and other security measures.

Living in Honduras **121**

Food Vocabulary

Leche	Milk
Jugo	Juice
Huevos	Eggs
Pan	Bread
Manzana	Apple
Pescado	Fish

Food

Rural Hondurans mainly eat corn, rice, and beans. Corn is made into tortillas and served with beans. Cassava, a starchy root, and plantains, a banana plant, are also common. Many poor Hondurans eat eggs regularly, but eat meat, fish, and rice only occasionally. They rarely eat green vegetables. In many villages, people raise pigs and chickens, but they are only eaten for special occasions. Wealthy Hondurans eat pork, beef, fruits, and vegetables more often.

Hondurans make large, flat bread out of cassava. It is especially popular among the Garífuna and the Pech.

There are several popular Honduran dishes. One of them is *sopa de mondongo*. This soup is made of beef innards, pig's feet, vegetables, and bread crumbs with a spiced tomato sauce base. *Tapado* is a coconut-milk soup with crab, clams, shrimp, fish heads, and plantains added. A homemade fermented corn drink is called *chicha*. Another drink, called *horchata*, is made from the *jícaro* tree. It is served during birthdays and holidays. But the national drink in Honduras is coffee.

For the middle and upper classes, a typical Honduran meal on the weekend includes beef, sausage or chicken, avocado, cheese, corn tortillas or rice, fried beans, and plantains. Sour cream is sometimes put on top of the fried beans or plantains or served on the side. During the week, a stew may replace the meat. Middle- and upper-class Hondurans eat beans, eggs, cheese or sour cream, and plantains for breakfast. Avocado is added only for lunch and dinner.

Corn tortillas are served at every meal. Because they are so important to the Honduran diet, San Pedro Sula's market has a lane called Tortilla Alley. Along this lane, people are making fresh tortillas in stall after stall. Hondurans can usually buy about forty tortillas for ten lempira.

Glory Bananas

Here's a recipe for a delicious dessert enjoyed by Hondurans.

Ingredients

2 tablespoons butter or margarine
4 very ripe medium-size bananas
2 tablespoons dark brown sugar
1 cinnamon stick, split in small pieces
1/4 cup milk

Directions

Melt the butter in a medium-size skillet over low heat. Add the peeled whole bananas. Sprinkle the brown sugar and cinnamon over the bananas. Pour the milk over the mixture. Cover the skillet and allow the bananas to cook at medium heat for about fifteen minutes. Uncover and cook for five more minutes, until the milk has evaporated and a thick syrup remains. Serve warm with a scoop of vanilla ice cream.

Among upper- and middle-class Hondurans, dating is closely supervised. Families will check into the backgrounds of any young men wanting to date their daughters. Engagements tend to be long, sometimes lasting several years.

Honduran president Ricardo Maduro got married in 2002. He is the first Honduran president ever to wed while in office.

Three types of marriages are accepted in Honduran society: civil marriage, religious marriage, and free unions. A civil marriage is performed by a government official in a government building. It is recognized by the government, and the couple is issued a marriage license. This type of marriage is common in Honduras in the lower class because it is inexpensive. In addition, if the couple wishes to divorce in the future, it is easy to do.

Religious marriage is done in a church and is presided over by a religious official such as a priest. This type of marriage is common among the middle and upper classes of Honduras. The ceremony can be quite expensive, and it is difficult to get a divorce from a religious marriage.

Among poorer people, many young couples live together in a free union rather than marry. Almost half of all Hondurans do this because of the expense of a marriage license and ceremony. Many eventually do marry, however.

Family Life

Honduran families work together to help one another survive and are very loyal. Because of this, outsiders are often viewed with suspicion. Families tend to be large, averaging almost four children per woman. Grandparents, aunts, and uncles sometimes all live in the same home. Families are the first place Hondurans look to in times of need, such as illness or job loss.

Men usually play the dominant role within the family. The father is a figure of authority and is respected by everyone in the household. Mothers are close to their children and openly affectionate. The mother runs the household affairs and is supposed to take care of her husband and family.

Honduran boys and girls are raised very differently, to prepare them for their adult life. Boys are allowed to do whatever they please and often go unwatched. Girls are constantly watched and are expected to be quiet and helpful.

Many people in the city are busy during the week. They set aside Sunday as a family day. Families eat meals together, and everyone can catch up on family news.

Honduran girls learn to help around the house from a young age. These girls are picking squash.

Holidays in Honduras

January 1	New Year's Day
April 14	Pan-American Day
May 1	Labor Day
September 15	Independence Day
October 3	Morazán Day
October 12	Discovery Day
October 21	Armed Forces Day

Life is slow and peaceful in rural Honduras.

Life in Rural Honduras

Daily life in rural Honduras is very different from the city. In small villages, the streets are dusty dirt roads. Pickup trucks thump as they hit speed bumps. Campesinos with guns or machetes hanging from their belts ride by on horseback. Cows, dogs, and chickens wander around. As the sun goes down, children ride bicycles and play in the street. Light spills from shopkeepers' homes as they peer out at passersby. Dogs bark and roosters crow. A seventeenth-century Catholic church shines in the dark. The noises of the night quiet down, and by ten o'clock, all is silent.

Before daybreak, dogs begin barking again, and then a rooster joins in. At 6:00 A.M., a bus trundles down the dirt roads, blasting its piercing horn to summon passengers.

Corn is the basis of breakfast. To prepare the meal, dry white corn is soaked in water and lime to soften it. Then it is placed in a hand grinder and ground into a soft, moist meal. Next it is placed on a flat stone and crushed with a stone rolling pin. The cornmeal is formed into perfectly round patties and cooked on a wood-burning stove. Coffee beans are also dried on top of the stove to prepare them.

In some places, women do laundry outside in a concrete basin. In other places, they take laundry to a river or stream to wash it while the children play and splash in the water.

Birthdays

Music and dance are important to any party in Honduras, including birthday parties. During the birthday party, cake, snacks, and drinks are served. Children may dress up in their finest clothes and play games. They get party boxes with candy and toys inside. Piñatas are central to many birthday parties. These large containers filled with candy or coins are hung from the ceiling. Children take turns hitting them with a stick or bat to try and break them open to spill the goodies onto the ground.

In the past, most Hondurans were named after a saint. Because of this, many people celebrated their saint's day as well as—or sometimes instead of—their own birthday. Today, more and more parents are giving their children other names. Slowly, life is changing in Honduras.

Sleepy Number

A popular game among children is called sleepy number. To play, the children form a big circle. One child gives each of the other children a number. Everyone holds hands and begins to go around and around. The child who assigned the numbers yells one out. The child with that number has to quickly yell out, "I'm not sleeping!" If the child with the number fails to yell that out, that child is sent to the center of the circle and must perform what the other children ask such as acting like a frog or an elephant. Then the circle begins going around and around again, another number is called out, and the fun goes on.

Timeline

Small groups of people roam   8000 B.C.
across Honduras.

The Maya build the great city of Copán.   A.D. 400s

Copán is abandoned.   800s

Christopher Columbus is the first European   1502
to reach what is now Honduras.

Hernán Cortés organizes a trip led by   1524
Cristóbal de Olid to explore Honduras.

Lempira, a Lenca chief who organized native   1537
resistance against the Spanish, is killed.

Central America declares its independence   1821
from Spain.

The United Provinces of Central America   1823
is formed.

World History

2500 B.C.   Egyptians build the Pyramids
and the Sphinx in Giza.

563 B.C.   The Buddha is born in India.

A.D. 313   The Roman emperor Constantine
recognizes Christianity.

610   The Prophet Muhammad begins preaching
a new religion called Islam.

1054   The Eastern (Orthodox) and Western
(Roman) Catholic Churches break apart.

1066   William the Conqueror defeats
the English in the Battle of Hastings.

1095   Pope Urban II proclaims the First Crusade.

1215   King John seals the Magna Carta.

1300s   The Renaissance begins in Italy.

1347   The Black Death sweeps through Europe.

1453   Ottoman Turks capture Constantinople,
conquering the Byzantine Empire.

1492   Columbus arrives in North America.

1500s   The Reformation leads to the birth
of Protestantism.

1776   The Declaration of Independence
is signed.

1789   The French Revolution begins.

Honduran History

Honduras leaves the United Provinces of Central America.	1838
Honduras adopts its first constitution.	1839
Honduras's first university is founded by Father José Trinidad Reyes in Tegucigalpa.	1847
Tegucigalpa becomes the capital of Honduras.	1880
The Vaccaro brothers ship their first boatload of bananas from Honduras to New Orleans.	1889
Honduras is the world's leading banana producer.	1925–1939
Workers at the United Fruit Company go on strike.	1954
President Ramón Villeda Morales is ousted in a bloody coup.	1963
The Soccer War breaks out between Honduras and El Salvador.	1969
Hurricane Fifi kills 8,000 people and wipes out the entire banana crop.	1974
The Honduran army ousts Colonel Oswaldo López Arellano, the nation's president.	1975
Democratic elections for a civilian government are held.	1981
The United States sets up military bases in Honduras.	1980s
Hurricane Mitch hits Honduras, causing about $4 billion worth of damage.	1998

World History

1865	American Civil War ends.
1914	World War I breaks out.
1917	The Bolshevik Revolution brings communism to Russia.
1929	Worldwide economic depression begins.
1939	World War II begins, following the German invasion of Poland.
1945	World War II ends.
1957	Vietnam War starts.
1969	Humans land on the moon.
1975	The Vietnam War ends.
1979	Soviet Union invades Afghanistan.
1983	Drought and famine in Africa.
1989	The Berlin Wall is torn down as communism crumbles in Eastern Europe.
1991	Soviet Union breaks into separate states.
1992	Bill Clinton is elected U.S. president.
2000	George W. Bush is elected U.S. president.
2001	Terrorists attack World Trade Center, New York, and the Pentagon, Washington, D.C.

Fast Facts

Official name: Republic of Honduras

Capital: Tegucigalpa

Official language: Spanish

Tegucigalpa

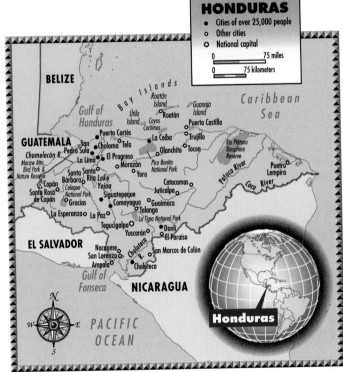

Honduras's flag

Pico Bonito

Major religion:	Roman Catholicism
Year of founding:	1838
National anthem:	*The National Anthem of Honduras*
Government:	Multiparty republic
Chief of state:	President
Area:	43,277 square miles (112,087 sq km)
Dimensions:	405 miles (652 km) from east to west
	240 miles (386 km) from north to south
Bordering countries:	Guatemala to the northwest, Nicaragua to the south, and El Salvador to the southwest
Highest elevation:	Cerro Las Minas, at 9,347 feet (2,849 m)
Lowest elevation:	Sea level along the coasts
Average annual rainfall:	30 inches (76 cm) in the central highlands; 100 inches (254 cm) in the Caribbean coastal region
National population (2005 est.):	6,975,204

Population of largest cities (2005 est.):

Tegucigalpa	850,848
San Pedro Sula	489,466
Choloma	139,800
La Ceiba	130,218
El Progreso	100,810

Copán Ruins

Currency

Famous landmarks: ▶ *Copán Ruins*, Copán

▶ *Río Plátano Biosphere Reserve,* northeastern plain

▶ *Church of Suyapa*, Tegucigalpa

▶ *Museum of Anthropology and History,* San Pedro Sula

▶ *National Art Gallery*, Tegucigalpa

▶ *Pico Bonito National Park*, La Ceiba

Industry: Service industries such as tourism make up the largest part of the Honduran economy. The manufacture of items such as palm oil, clothing, and wood products is also important. Agriculture accounts for about 13 percent of the Honduran economy. Sugarcane, coffee, corn, bananas, and shrimp are widely grown.

Currency: The Honduran lempira is Honduras's basic unit of currency. In 2006, about 19 lempiras was equal to 1 U.S. dollar.

System of weights and measures: A combination of the metric system and an old Spanish-pound system called libras

Literacy (2003): 76 percent

Honduran schoolgirls

Francisco Morazán

Common words and phrases:

Hola	Hello
Adiós	Good-bye
Buenos días	Good morning
Buenas tardes	Good afternoon
Buenas noches	Good evening
¿Cómo estás?	How are you?
Muy bien	Very good
Gracias	Thank you
De nada	You're welcome
Sí	Yes
No	No
Perdóneme	Excuse me
Por favor	Please

Famous Hondurans:

José Cecilio Del Valle (1776–1834)
Author of the Central American declaration of independence

Lempira (1499–1537)
Lenca chief

Francisco Morazán (1792–1842)
President of the United Provinces of Central America

José Trinidad Reyes (1797–1855)
Priest, poet, playwright, and founder of the National Autonomous University of Honduras

Pablo Zelaya Sierra (1896–1933)
Father of the Honduran modern art movement

To Find Out More

Books

▶ Deedrick, Tami. *Ancient Civilizations: Maya.* New York: Raintree Steck-Vaughn, 2001.

▶ Foster, Lynn V. *A Brief History of Central America.* New York: Facts on File, 2000.

▶ Marx, Jennifer. *Pirates and Privateers of the Caribbean.* Malabar, Fla.: Krieger, 1992.

▶ McGaffey, Leta. *Honduras.* New York: Marshall Cavendish, 1999.

▶ Merrick, Patrick. *Honduras.* Chanhassen, Minn.: Child's World, 2001.

Web Sites

▶ **Embassy of the United States of America in Tegucigalpa, Honduras**
http://honduras.usembassy.gov/english/index_e1.htm
Information page on current issues, crime and security matters, and other subjects.

▶ **Encarta: Honduras**
http://encarta.msn.com/encyclopedia_761563646/Honduras.html
Gives an overview of Honduran geography, people, resources, history, and more.

▶ **NationMaster: History of Honduras**
http://www.nationmaster.com/encyclopedia/History-of-Honduras
Contains a detailed look at Honduran history.

Embassy

▶ **Embassy of Honduras**
3007 Tilden Street NW
Suite 4M
Washington, DC 20008
202-966-7702

Index

Meet the Author

Sara Louise Kras's love for travel began when she was a little girl. Her mother would take the family to the amazing national parks in the United States. She continued the tradition of travel as she got older. She has lived in Zimbabwe, South Africa, and England. In addition, she has explored Australia, Kenya, Thailand, Cambodia, Maldives, Japan, Costa Rica, Honduras, Mexico, Canada, Denmark, and France.

While visiting Honduras, she talked to government officials about their country. She visited the mountainous region of Tegucigalpa and Gracias. She walked through the Copán ruins, swam in the Caribbean Sea off the coast of Roatán, and hiked through the rain forest of Pico Bonito. Her favorite part of Honduras was staying with two old Honduran women in a small town called San Juan. Campesinos wandered on horseback through the dusty streets, and friendly children asked her name in Spanish. Another exciting event was attending a guancasco in La Campa. She was thrilled to watch the dancer with the mask, whip, and stuffed iguana, and to listen to the drummer and flute player, while excited religious followers carried the saint upon their shoulders.

Sara grew up in Washington State, Texas, and Colorado. She has always loved the outdoors. She enjoys exploring nature and seeing animals in their natural habitat. She currently lives in Glendale, California, with her husband and her cat, Gigi. Sara is the author of more than fifteen books for children.

"I have always been fascinated with other cultures and ways of life," she says. "Seeing people live a completely different lifestyle to what I am used to makes me appreciate what we have. Finding out about these cultures and then telling children about them is one of my favorite things to do. I love to get children excited about the world they live in and to get them curious to find out more."

Photo Credits